THE FAR RIGHT TODAY

To my readers,
in the hope that this book
will educate and empower you

THE FAR RIGHT TODAY

Cas Mudde

polity

First published in 2019 by Polity Press
Reprinted 2019 (five times), 2020 (twice), 2021

Polity Press
65 Bridge Street
Cambridge CB2 1UR, UK

Polity Press
101 Station Landing
Suite 300
Medford, MA 02155, USA

ISBN-13: 978-1-5095-3683-2
ISBN-13: 978-1-5095-3684-9 (pb)

A catalogue record for this book is available from the British Library.

Typeset in 11 on 13 pt Sabon
by Fakenham Prepress Solutions, Fakenham, Norfolk NR21 8NL
Printed and bound in the United States by LSC Communications

The publisher has used its best endeavours to ensure that the URLs for external websites referred to in this book are correct and active at the time of going to press. However, the publisher has no responsibility for the websites and can make no guarantee that a site will remain live or that the content is or will remain appropriate.

Every effort has been made to trace all copyright holders, but if any have been overlooked the publisher will be pleased to include any necessary credits in any subsequent reprint or edition.

For further information on Polity, visit our website:
politybooks.com

Contents

Acknowledgments

Throughout my career, I have had the great fortune of receiving generous support from many wonderful colleagues and friends in the academic field of extremism and democracy. For this particular book, which has a much broader geographical and topical scope than my more narrow academic work, I called upon an exceptionally broad range of them for feedback and was yet again humbled by their response. Aurelien Mondon, Caterina Froio, Cristóbal Rovira Kaltwasser, Cynthia Miller-Idriss, Duncan McDonnell, George Hawley, Jan-Werner Müller, Kathleen Blee, Léonie de Jonge, Matthew Feldman, and Uwe Backes all read the first full manuscript and provided me with many smaller and bigger suggestions. I was able to include several of them, but was forced to ignore some, because of the practical constraints of this relatively short book.

Special thanks go out to four more people. Alex DiBranco was able and willing to read over the later added chapter on gender and provided me with crucial feedback within a week. My amazing wife Maryann Gallagher not only facilitated my writing but also read an earlier draft of the gender chapter and helped me reshape and rethink it. My fantastic graduate student Jakub Wondreys did vital research assistance for the book and helped me construct the chronology and the glossary. He also read through the full manuscript and provided me with helpful comments. I thank him for all his work and cannot wait to repay it, by editing his dissertation. Finally, a shout out to my friend and publisher Craig Fowlie, who made time in his extremely busy schedule to provide me with great feedback on the full manuscript, despite the fact that it is published by a competitor. Perhaps he is right after all: Scousers are special.

I have written several books before, some purely academic, some mostly non-academic. In most cases, I acted quite quickly on the initial idea, but it then took me a (very) long time to turn it into a book. This book is the exact opposite. I have been brooding over this idea for more than a decade, returning to it each time I was asked for a recommendation for a relatively short, non-academic book after giving a public lecture. But once I approached Polity with the idea, the book almost wrote itself – if I could find time for it in between family, lectures, meetings, teaching, and travel. I want to thank the three anonymous referees for their constructive and encouraging reviews and my editors at Polity, Louise Knight and Sophie Wright, for their quick and hands-on editing style. It confirmed my long-held feeling that Polity is indeed the perfect publisher for this book.

Abbreviations

AfD	Alternative for Germany
ANS/NA	Action Front of National Socialists/ National Activists
APF	Alliance for Peace and Freedom
B&H	Blood & Honour
BJP	Indian People's Party
DF	Danish People's Party
EAF	European Alliance for Freedom
EDL	English Defence League
EKRE	Conservative People's Party of Estonia
ENF	Europe of Nations and Freedom
ESM	European Social Movement
FN	National Front (France)
FPÖ	Austrian Freedom Party
FvD	Forum for Democracy
GRECE	Research and Study Group for European Civilization
KKK	Ku Klux Klan
LN	Northern League
LPR	League of Polish Families
L'SNS	Kotleba – People's Party Our Slovakia
MHP	Nationalist Action Party
MSI	Italian Social Movement
NF	National Front (UK)

NMR	Nordic Resistance Movement
NPD	National Democratic Party of Germany
ONP	One Nation Party
PEGIDA	Patriotic Europeans Against the Islamization of the Occident
PiS	Law and Justice
PVV	Party for Freedom
REP	The Republicans
RN	National Rally
RSS	National Volunteer Organization
SD	Sweden Democrats
SNS	Slovak National Party
SRP	Socialist Reich Party
SVP	Swiss People's Party
UKIP	United Kingdom Independence Party
VB	Flemish Bloc/Flemish Interest
XA	Golden Dawn

Introduction

On a grey and drizzly day in January 2017, on the steps of the Capitol Building in Washington, DC, the newly elected president of the United States gave a speech unlike any of his predecessors. It had the anger and frustration of the political fringes, but it came from the political mainstream. In his inaugural speech, the new "Leader of the Free World" said:

> For too long, a small group in our nation's Capital has reaped the rewards of government while the people have borne the cost. Washington flourished – but the people did not share in its wealth. Politicians prospered – but the jobs left, and the factories closed. The establishment protected itself, but not the citizens of our country. Their victories have not been your victories; their triumphs have not been your triumphs; and while they celebrated in our nation's Capital, there was little to celebrate for struggling families all across our land. That all changes – starting right here, and right now, because this moment is your moment: it belongs to you.

The election of Donald Trump is in many ways illustrative of what this book is about: the mainstreaming and normalization of the far right in general, and the populist radical right in particular, in the twenty-first century. As I finish this manuscript, in May 2019, three of the five most populous countries in the world have a far-right leader (Brazil, India, and the US) and the biggest political party in the world is the populist radical right Indian People's Party (BJP). Within the European Union (EU), two governments are fully controlled by populist radical right parties (Hungary and Poland), another four include such parties (Bulgaria, Estonia, Italy, Slovakia), and two are held up with support of a populist right party (Denmark and the United Kingdom).[1] And in the latest European elections, far-right parties increased their presence in the European Parliament yet again, albeit modestly, as they had done in the previous elections in 2014 and 2009.

A lot has changed since I started working on the far right in the late 1980s, as a student at the University of Leiden in the Netherlands, when the far right was still primarily a phenomenon of the political margins. Neo-Nazi groups could barely protest in the streets without being arrested and anti-immigration parties barely registered in the polls. Today, the far right is closely connected to the political mainstream; and in more and more countries it is becoming the political mainstream. Let me illustrate this disturbing transformation with three (European) examples.

In 1982, thousands of protesters filled the square in front of the Dutch parliament in The Hague. Carrying signs that read "They Are Back" and "Racism is Hate Against Humans," they protested against one man, Hans Janmaat, leader of the misnamed Center Party, who, with fewer than 70,000 votes (0.8 percent), had entered the Second Chamber. Fast-forward more than three decades, and the Dutch parliament counts twenty-two (out of 150) far-right Members of Parliament (MPs), installed without any protests, while the main right-wing government parties advance and implement policies that are fully anchored in the Center Party's main point of controversy: "The Netherlands is not an immigration country. Stop immigration!"

In 1999, the Austrian Freedom Party (FPÖ) gained its biggest electoral success to date, coming second with 26.9 percent of the vote in the parliamentary elections. When the party entered the government the next year, it was met by mass demonstrations and an international boycott. When the FPÖ returned to government in 2018, few Austrians came out to demonstrate, while the international community embraced the coalition with virtually no protest.

And, finally, in France, most French people responded with horror when the leader of the National Front (FN), Jean-Marie Le Pen, made the 2002 presidential run-offs with 16.9 percent of the national vote. In response, turnout for the second round increased substantially, keeping Le Pen at 17.8 percent, less than one percent higher than in the first round. Fifteen years later, his daughter Marine made the second round with 21.3 percent. This time (even) fewer French people voted in the second round and Le Pen increased her support to 33.9 percent. With Marine Le Pen almost doubling her father's 2002 score, most French people were relieved rather than upset. At least she didn't win.

These examples illustrate the fundamental differences between the so-called "third wave" and "fourth wave" of the postwar far right. The third wave, roughly from 1980 till 2000, saw the rise of electorally successful populist radical right parties, although they were largely reduced to the political margins, as mainstream parties excluded them from political coalitions and often minimized "their" issues, notably immigration and European integration. In the fourth wave, which roughly started in the twenty-first century, radical right parties have become mainstreamed and increasingly normalized, not just in Europe, but across the world. And even extreme right parties have emerged, as extreme right sentiments (like antisemitism, historical revisionism, and racism) are openly flirted with in the media and politics.

The so-called "refugee crisis" of 2015 played a special role in this development. I put the term in quotes because whether or not it was indeed a crisis is more a matter of personal judgment than objective condition. The EU had the financial resources to deal with even these record numbers of asylum seekers, although for years it had neglected to build an infrastructure to properly take care of them. Mainstream media and politicians *chose* to frame the influx of asylum seekers as a "crisis," thereby providing ammunition to the already mobilized far right.

The "refugee crisis" was not the initial cause of the mainstreaming of the far right, in Europe or beyond, but it has definitely functioned as a catalyst for the process. Anti-immigration demonstrations have become a common occurrence on the streets of major European cities, while far-right violence against anti-fascists, immigrants, the LGBTQ community, and refugees has increased sharply. From Germany to the US, law enforcement and intelligence agencies warn of a growing far-right terrorist danger, often after decades of downplaying this threat.

This book aims to give an accessible and concise overview of the fourth wave of the postwar far right. While it includes several original observations which will also be of interest to more expert readers, this book is first and foremost written for a non-academic audience; for people who follow the news, are concerned about the rise of the far right, but feel that media accounts provide too little detail and insight, while academic and non-academic books are too complex or simply too long. It draws on more than a quarter-century of scholarship, including my own, and simplifies and summarizes this in ten clearly structured chapters.

My hope is that after reading this book, the reader will feel better equipped to assess the key challenges that the far right poses to liberal democracies in the twenty-first century and to feel empowered to defend liberal democracy against these challenges. But before she can do this, we have to address one of the most confusing and frustrating aspects of the academic and public debate on the topic: terminology.

Terminology

The ideas and groups at the heart of this book are described with an ever-growing myriad of terms, often used interchangeably, yet without a clear definition or explanation of the differences and similarities. While issues of terminology might sound like a purely academic matter, they are crucial to politics and the public debate. For instance, in countries like Germany, "extreme right" groups can be banned, while "radical right" groups cannot.

It is true that most of the defining and terming is done by outsiders, that is, academics, anti-fascists, and journalists, rather than by the far right itself, but this is not to say that it does not care about terminology. Leaders from prominent far-right parties, like the FN (now National Rally, RN) and FPÖ, have taken academics and journalists to court for describing them as "fascist," for example. Others have proudly proclaimed themselves to be populists, and sometimes even racist, albeit often after redefining the term more favorably. For example, Matteo Salvini, leader of the Northern League (LN; now just League) and Italy's interior minister, said that while "populist" was used as an insult, for him, it was a compliment. And former Breitbart News CEO and Trump advisor Steve Bannon told FN activists at a party gathering, "Let them call you racists. Let them call you xenophobes. Let them call you nativists. Wear it as a badge of honor."

There is no academic consensus on the correct terms for the broader movement and the various subgroups within it. Moreover, the dominant term has been changing throughout the postwar era. In the first decades, these movements were primarily described in terms of "neo-fascism," which changed to "extreme right" in the 1980s, "radical right" in the 1990s, some form of "right-wing populism" in the early twenty-first century, as well as "far right" in more recent years. This development reflects changes both within the movement itself and in the scholarly community that studies it.

Most academics agree that the movement is part of the broader *right*, but disagree over what that exactly means. The terms "left" and "right" date back to the French Revolution (1789–99), when supporters of the king sat to the right of the president of the French parliament and opponents to the left. This means that those on the right were in favor of the *ancien régime*, marked by its hierarchical order, while those on the left supported democratization and popular sovereignty. After the Industrial Revolution, the left–right division became mainly defined in terms of socio-economic policies, with the right supporting a free market and the left a more active role of the state, although alternative meanings remained popular – such as religious (right) versus secular (left). In more recent decades, left–right has become more defined in socio-cultural terms, with the right standing for either authoritarianism (versus the left's libertarianism) or nationalism (versus the left's internationalism) – or, in the terms of RN leader Marine Le Pen, "patriot–globalist."

While these various interpretations differ on many points, they do share an essential core, which has been captured most accurately by the Italian philosopher Norberto Bobbio,[2] who defines the key distinction between left and right on the basis of their view on (in) equality: the *left* considers the key inequalities between people to be artificial and negative, which should be overcome by an active state, whereas the *right* believes that inequalities between people are natural and positive, and should be either defended or left alone by the state. These inequalities can be (believed to be) cultural, economic, racial, religious, or however defined.

This book is not concerned with the so-called "mainstream right," such as conservatives and liberals/libertarians, but only with those on the right who are "anti-system," defined here as hostile to liberal democracy. This is what I call the *far right*, which is itself divided into two broader subgroups. The *extreme right* rejects the essence of democracy, that is, popular sovereignty and majority rule. The most infamous example of the extreme right is fascism, which brought to power German *Führer* Adolf Hitler and Italian *Duce* Benito Mussolini, and was responsible for the most destructive war in world history. The *radical right* accepts the essence of democracy, but opposes funda-mental elements of *liberal* democracy, most notably minority rights, rule of law, and separation of powers. Both subgroups oppose the postwar liberal democratic consensus, but in fundamentally different ways. While the extreme right is revolutionary, the radical right is more reformist. In essence, the radical right trusts the power of the people, the extreme right does not.

Given the prevalence of the term *populism* in contem-porary political discussions, let me quickly clarify both my understanding of that term and its relationship to the far right. I define populism as a (thin) ideology that considers society to be ultimately separated into two homogeneous and antagonistic groups, the pure people and the corrupt elite, and which argues that politics should be an expression of the *volonté générale* (general will) of the people (see also chapter 2). At least in theory, populism is pro-democracy, but anti-liberal democracy. Consequently, the extreme right is, by definition, not populist, while the radical right can be – and, in the twenty-first century, predominantly is.

Outline of the Book

This book focuses predominantly on the fourth wave, that is, on the far right in the twenty-first century. While I aim to present the far right in its diversity, including both the extreme right and the radical right, the emphasis will be on the most important ideas, organizations, and personalities of the contemporary period, that is, populist radical right leaders and parties. The first set of chapters focuses primarily on the far right itself (chapters 1–5), while the second deals with the far right within the (mostly western democratic) political context (chapters 6–8).

Chapter 1 provides a concise chronological overview of the four waves of postwar far-right politics. Chapter 2 introduces the key ideologies and issues of the contemporary far right. Chapter 3 focuses on the organizational structure of the far right, distinguishing between far-right parties, social movement organizations, and subcultures. Chapter 4 shifts the focus to the people within the far right, more specifically leaders, members and activists, and voters. Chapter 5 examines the main forms of mobilization, that is, elections, demonstrations, and violence.

The next three chapters situate the far right within its (western democratic) political context. Chapters 6 and 7 discuss the causes and consequences of the recent rise of the far right, summarizing some of the key academic and public debates – such as economic anxiety versus cultural backlash – and highlighting the broad variety of far-right challenges that western democracies are facing today. Chapter 8 reviews the different ways in which democracies have responded to the rise of the far right. Chapter 9 looks at the role of gender within the far right, relating it to most of the aspects discussed in the previous chapters. Finally, chapter 10 ends the book with twelve theses that highlight key characteristics and novelties of the fourth wave of the postwar far right.

1

History

In 1945, the world started to recover from the second world war in thirty years. An estimated 75 to 85 million people were killed, and many more were seriously injured. Europe was in ruins. Nazi Germany and the Soviet Union bore the brunt of the destruction, but almost all European countries were severely affected by collaboration, destruction, and occupation. Millions of minorities had perished in the Nazi annihilation and concentration camps, most notably Jews, Roma and Sinti (commonly referred to by the derogatory term "Gypsies"), homosexuals, and communists.

As the European continent was recovering from one division, between fascists and anti-fascists, it was entering another one, between communists and anti-communists. The Cold War separated Europe into a capitalist and (largely) democratic West and a socialist and authoritarian East. This division preceded the Second World War, and the two sides were only brought together by the shared threat of fascism, because anti-fascism was one of the few values communists and liberal democrats shared (despite the cynical pact that

Hitler and Stalin struck between 1939 and 1941). Yet, as soon as fascism was destroyed, the two became mortal enemies again.

The anti-fascist consensus would survive the Cold War, even though there were fundamental national and regional differences in the ways in which countries dealt with the far right in the postwar era. In communist states, all "fascist" ideas and movements were banned, as were all other non-communist ideas and movements. Most East European collaborators and fascists were killed in the war and the postwar repression or were able to escape to, primarily, the Americas, where they integrated into broader anti-communist émigré communities, which often already held very right-wing ideas.

While most western democracies also went through a short period of, partly extrajudicial and violent, repression of local fascists and collaborators, particularly in countries that were occupied by Nazi Germany, many had more ambivalent legal restrictions on far-right ideas and movements. Countries that had not been occupied, like the UK and US, introduced virtually no restrictions, while others, notably Germany and Italy, officially banned "neo-fascist" ideas and movements (see chapter 8). Despite different legal systems, and social pressures, the general lesson of the Second World War was "never again." It was a sentiment that was also at the heart of the process of European integration, which aimed to integrate economies and pool sovereignty to create a bulwark against nationalism.

Three Waves of the Postwar Far Right, 1945–2000

In 1988, the German political scientist Klaus von Beyme[1] identified three waves of far-right politics in postwar Western Europe. While there is some debate about the exact characteristics and time periods of the different waves, his model does provide at least a rough sketch of the ways in which the far right fared in the second half of the twentieth century.

Neo-Fascism, 1945–55

In the direct aftermath of the defeat of fascism, far-right politics was backward- rather than forward-looking. Given that almost all far-right activists and groups had collaborated with the fascists during the war, far-right politics was almost universally rejected – and in some countries, like Germany and the Netherlands, all nationalisms were perceived negatively. Most Europeans who had either ideologically supported, or opportunistically collaborated with, the fascist regimes adapted to the new democratic reality either by becoming apolitical or by working within the democratic parties and system.

The small group of fascists who remained loyal to the cause, and who were not or no longer imprisoned, worked mainly at the margins of society. They were mostly described as "neo-fascists," but there was really not much new to them. They were old fascists who remained loyal to the old ideology, who organized primarily within social organizations, providing camaraderie and social support for the "heroes" and martyrs" of the fascist cause. Among the more important groups were those providing support for former Eastern Front fighters (mostly Waffen-SS) and their families, such as the Belgian Saint-Martin Fund and the German Mutual Aid Association of Former Waffen-SS Soldiers – millions of children and wives had lost their fathers and husbands and were left without a state pension because their countries considered them traitors.

As far as (neo-)fascists wanted to remain politically active, they had to operate in a hostile legal and political climate. Even when cautious not to be openly neo-fascist, far-right organizations led by former (high-ranking) fascists rarely achieved popular support and often faced significant state repression. Most of the political parties did not contest elections, and even if they did, they would remain well under the electoral threshold of parliamentary representation. Several (neo-)fascist parties were banned in the 1950s, including the German Socialist Reich Party (SRP) in 1952 and the Dutch National European Social Movement in 1956.

The main exception was the Italian Social Movement (MSI), which was led by a former Fascist government official, Giorgio Almirante, and made little secret of its credentials – the initials allegedly signified "*Mussolini Sei Immortale*" (Mussolini, You Are Immortal). Although the new Italian Constitution explicitly stated, "It shall be forbidden to reorganize, under any form whatsoever, the dissolved Fascist party," the MSI entered parliament in 1948 and remained represented until its transformation into the "post-fascist" National Alliance in 1995. It even provided parliamentary support for the short-lived Tambroni government in 1960.

Outside of Europe, neo-fascist ideas were often represented in East European émigré organizations in the Americas and Australia. This was strengthened by the influx of former fascist activists and politicians, particularly from collaborationist regimes in Croatia, Hungary, and Slovakia, after the end of the Second World War. In Latin America, some more or less relevant groups were strongly influenced by the far-right regimes of Antonio Salazar's Estado Novo in Portugal and, in particular, Francisco Franco's Falange in Spain.

In an attempt to break away from their national marginalization, some fascist leaders tried to organize at the international level. The most famous attempt was the European Social Movement (ESM), inspired by the success of the MSI, which was founded at a congress in Malmö (Sweden) in 1951. While it brought together the most well-known far-right activists of that period, as well as representatives of the most relevant far-right parties (including the MSI and SRP), the ESM remained marginal in its short life, becoming moribund in 1957. The same applied to all other attempts at far-right collaboration, including the various attempts to develop a European nationalism by people like the British fascist Oswald Mosley (also involved in the ESM) and the US attorney and polemicist Francis Parker Yockey, founder of the ambitiously named European Liberation Front, which existed from 1949 till 1954.

Right-Wing Populism, 1955–80

Small neo-fascist groups continued to exist on the margins of western societies, but the ensuing decades saw the rise of a variety of right-wing populist parties and politicians, which were defined by opposition to the postwar elites rather than allegiance to a defeated ideology and regime. Former fascists played a role in many of these parties, but they were not neo-fascist in terms of either ideology or personnel. First and foremost, these parties revolted against postwar conditions, most notably the marginalization of the rural peripheries and the development of the welfare state.

While there had been some earlier right-wing populist parties, like the National Agricultural Party in Ireland and the Common Man's Front in Italy in the 1940s, the defining movement was the Defense Union of Shopkeepers and Craftsmen, better known as the Poujadists, after its leader Pierre Poujade. Poujadism did include several features of fascism, including a strong focus on the leader and a strident anti-parliamentarism – Poujade called the *Assemblée Nationale* "the biggest brothel in Paris" – but was not openly anti-democratic.

It became a mass movement almost overnight, counting some 400,000 members in 1955, and gaining fifty-two seats in the 1956 elections under the name of Union and French Fraternity. When General Charles de Gaulle founded the Fifth Republic in 1958, the Poujadists quickly disappeared from French politics, although they would leave an important legacy: Jean-Marie Le Pen was the leader of its youth movement and was elected as the youngest parliamentarian in French postwar history in 1956 (a feat his granddaughter, Marion Maréchal-Le Pen, would repeat in 2012).

There were similar rural populist parties after the Poujadists, most notably the Farmers' Party in the Netherlands, but the most important right-wing populist parties that emerged later in the second wave had a different profile. In 1973, the Progress Party took the Danish political establishment by surprise, scoring 15.9 percent of the vote in its first-ever election – the party was founded just the previous year by the idiosyncratic lawyer and TV personality Mogens Glistrup. Also in 1973, a similar party, initially named Anders Lange's Party for a Strong Reduction in Taxes, Duties, and Public Intervention but renamed Progress Party in 1977, gained a more modest 5 percent in Norway. Both Progress Parties are best described as "neoliberal populist," however, railing against high taxes and big government – the Danish party wanted to scrap defense altogether, presenting as its policy an answering machine message stating "we surrender" in Russian.

In addition, some new far-right parties were founded that were hybrids, that is, combinations of old extreme right (often neo-fascist) and new radical right ideas and personnel. Possibly the first such party was the Swiss National Action for People and Nation, founded in 1961, but the most important, and enduring, was the National Democratic Party of Germany (NPD), founded in 1964. While founded by former Nazi officials, the

NPD focused primarily on postwar issues, including the most important theme of the future: non-European immigration. Similarly, the British National Front (NF), a crudely racist party, founded from a merger of smaller groups in 1967, had some localized impact in the late 1970s organizing behind slogans like "Stop Immigration" and "Make Britain Great Again."

In the United States, right-wing populism mainly operated within the broader anti-communist movement, whose most (in)famous representatives were the John Birch Society and Senator Joseph McCarthy. It got a second wind in the presidential campaign of Republican Senator Barry Goldwater, which ended disastrously, but provided the germ for the birth of a new, more radical, conservative subculture. The most significant radical right moment, however, was the 1968 presidential run of Alabama governor George Wallace, under the heading of the American Independent Party. Running on an explicitly racist agenda, vehemently defending racial segregation, Wallace was the only third-party candidate to win states in the postwar era – indeed he won no less than five, all in the former confederate South. This was part of a broader racist opposition to desegregation in the former Confederate states, which included the infamous Ku Klux Klan (KKK), which had flourished twice before, in the late 1860s and 1920s, and now, in its third iteration, grew back to roughly 50,000 people in the 1960s, as well as the more respectable Citizens' Council, with an estimated membership of ca. 250,000.

Radical Right, 1980–2000

The first significant wave of far-right politics in Western Europe started in the early 1980s, picking up real steam only in the 1990s. Fueled by unemployment and mass immigration, although with a lag effect of almost a decade, radical right parties started to slowly but steadily enter national parliaments. The earliest was the Flemish Bloc (VB), which entered the Belgian parliament as an electoral alliance in 1978, followed by the Dutch Center Party in 1982. Both parties had modest support, around 1 percent, translating into one representative in the highly proportional electoral systems of their respective countries. In 1986, the French FN, which had been founded fourteen years earlier and had so far contested national elections unsuccessfully, profited from a change in the electoral system to translate its 9.6 percent of the vote into thirty-five parliamentary seats. Two years later, France changed back to its previous majoritarian system, which accomplished what it meant to do: the FN scored an identical percentage, but gained zero seats.

In addition to various new radical right parties, such as The Republicans in Germany and the Sweden Democrats (SD), the third wave included former mainstream parties, such as the FPÖ in Austria and the Swiss People's Party (SVP), which were transformed into populist radical right parties by new (official or unofficial) party leaders – Jörg Haider and Christoph Blocher, respectively. These parties proved much more durable than previous far-right parties – the MSI excluded – and, with some exceptions, remain relevant today.

After the fall of communism in 1989, the far right also emerged in various post-communist countries, although initially in more specifically regional forms. It included parties like the Croatian Party of Rights and the Slovak National Party (SNS), which harked back in ideology and even some personnel to fascist parties of the 1930s and 1940s, as well as parties that merged far-right features with communist nostalgia, like the Greater Romania Party. At the same time, far-right politicians got elected on lists of non-far-right parties, such as the Bulgarian Socialist Party, the Communist Party of the Russian Federation, and Solidarity Electoral Action in Poland.

By the turn of the century, the populist radical right had become the dominant ideology within the European far right. Although there were national and regional differences – for example, opposition to non-European immigration was less important in the East, while opposition to Roma was mostly absent in the West – almost all relevant far-right parties combined nativism, authoritarianism, and populism (see chapter 2). They railed against immigrants and/or indigenous minorities as well as European and national elites, while presenting themselves as the voice of the people who said what the people think.

Only a few populist radical right parties contested elections in the 1980s, scoring on average just 2.3 percent in the countries in which they participated – 1.1 percent in Europe overall. By contrast, most European countries had at least one far-right party contesting elections in the 1990s, gaining on average 4.4 percent (see the table below). The differences between Eastern and Western Europe were significantly smaller than was generally assumed, although the highest score in Eastern Europe was much higher than in Western Europe: 45.2 percent in Croatia versus 26.9 percent in Switzerland.

While electoral and organizational volatility was high, with parties emerging and disappearing rapidly, particularly in the extremely unstable party systems of Eastern Europe, several populist radical right parties started to establish themselves within national political systems in the 1990s. For instance, the FN, LN, and VB all became part of the established parties in their respective countries, even if they mostly remained outside of the political establishment. Owing to still limited electoral success, however, as well as ideological, personal, and

Average vote for far-right parties in national parliamentary elections in EU member states, 1980–2018 (by decade)

Years	Average vote (%)	No. countries	No. parties
1980–9	1.1	17	8
1990–9	4.4	28	24
2000–9	4.7	28	24
2010–18	7.5	28	34

Note: The averages of the table are based on the twenty-eight countries that were members of the European Union in 2018. The score for the 1980s only reflects West European states, as Eastern Europe was still under communist rule at that time.
Source: Parlgov.

tactical differences, the European far right was largely unable to come together transnationally. Political groups in the European Parliament tended to include only some parties, and were short-lived because of disagreements within and between them (see chapter 3).

Outside of Europe, far-right parties started to become important players within the fragmented Israeli party system – with parties like Moledet and Tkuma, which entered parliament as part of the electoral alliance National Union in 1999. And while the neo-fascist Kach party of Rabbi Meir Kahane, as well as its successor Kahane Lives, were banned by the state in 1994, Kahanism would become the dominant strand in the Israeli far right in the fourth wave. In South Africa, openly racist organizations like the Afrikaner Resistance Movement lost support after the end of the apartheid regime in 1994, spiraling increasingly into an orgy of political violence.

Far-right groups existed only on the margins in the US, although some politicians tried to build a basis within the Republican Party – such as former KKK Grand

Wizard David Duke and "paleoconservative" journalist and politician Patrick "Pat" Buchanan. In Australia, Pauline Hanson was elected as an Independent in 1996 after the Liberal Party of Australia had disendorsed her because of derogatory remarks about Indigenous Australians. The following year, she founded her One Nation Party (ONP), which had some initial successes, but also suffered much internal division and strife. Most prominently, in 1980, the BJP was founded in India on the basis of the Bharatiya Jana Sangh and Janata Party, which would soon challenge the dominance of the hegemonic Congress Party.

The Fourth Wave, 2000–

The far right entered a fourth wave in the twenty-first century, electorally and politically profiting from three "crises": the terrorist attacks of September 11, 2001 (and beyond), the Great Recession of 2008, and the "refugee crisis" of 2015. All the western democracies were affected, albeit in different ways, shaking the national and international political status quo, and giving rise to an unprecedented wave of Islamophobic and populist protest.

What characterizes the fourth wave, and differentiates it from the third wave, is the mainstreaming of the far right. While far-right politics was largely considered out of bounds for mainstream parties and politicians after 1945, with some notable exceptions (such as Eastern Europe in the 1990s and the US South in the 1960s), this is no longer the case today. In more and more countries, populist radical right parties and politicians are considered *koalitionsfähig* (acceptable for coalitions) by mainstream right, and sometimes even left, parties. Moreover, populist radical right (and even some extreme right) ideas are openly debated in mainstream circles, while populist radical right policies are adopted, albeit it generally in (slightly) more moderate form, by mainstream parties.

Another characteristic of the fourth wave is the heterogeneity of the far right, even within the subgroup of successful political parties. While the usual suspects still constitute the core – that is, the populist radical right parties that emerge from outside the political mainstream – they are complemented by a dizzying array of new far-right parties. The most important are transformed conservative parties, such as the Alliance of Young Democrats–Hungarian Civic Alliance (Fidesz) and Law and Justice (PiS) in Poland. Western European mainstream parties had transformed into radical right parties before, but the FPÖ and the SVP did this in opposition, while Fidesz and PiS transformed while in government. Even more shocking is the emergence of extreme right parties in national parliaments, such as the neo-Nazi Golden Dawn (XA) in Greece and the People's Party – Our Slovakia (L'SNS), which was renamed Kotleba – People's Party Our Slovakia in 2015, after its leader Marian Kotleba.

Even when limiting our analysis to populist radical right parties, that is, the usual suspects, we see a fundamental change in the twenty-first century. First of all, most of the parties significantly increased their support. Far-right parties gained on average 4.7 percent of the vote in the first decade of the twenty-first century, and 7.5 percent in the second, that is, 2010–18 (see the table above). Second, populist radical right parties broke through in countries that had previously resisted them, like Germany and Sweden, or where they had remained relatively marginal, like Hungary and the Netherlands. Third, many populist radical right parties have numbered among the biggest parties in their country. In fact, several parties are, or have been at one time, the biggest party in their country in nationwide elections and polls, including the Danish People's Party (DF), Fidesz, the FN, PiS, and the SVP.

Radical right parties also became more relevant for government formation. First and foremost, more and more parties entered government, and in a variety of ways. Some, like Fidesz and PiS, were able to constitute governments by themselves – something only the Croatian Democratic Union[2] had been able to achieve in the third wave. Several others became official partners in coalition governments with non-far-right parties, such as the FPÖ in Austria, National Union Attack in Bulgaria, Popular Orthodox Rally in Greece, and LN in Italy. Finally, a few parties supported minority governments of non-far-right parties, generally getting a stricter immigration policy in return – as was the case with the DF in Denmark (2001–11 as well as 2016–19) and the Party for Freedom (PVV) in the Netherlands (2010–12).

And while the far right already had agenda-setting power during the third wave, leading often to a tougher discourse on immigration and immigrants, though more rarely to a toughening of policies, this has increased significantly during the fourth wave (see chapter 7). In the wake of the three "crises" of the early twenty-first century, radical right politics has become largely detached from populist radical right parties. Many (right-wing) parties now advance a nativist, authoritarian, and populist discourse, including Euroscepticism, Islamophobia, and opposition to "do-goodism" and "political correctness." From Austrian chancellor Sebastian Kurz to his British counterpart Theresa May, mainstream politicians are no longer just paying lip service to populist radical right policies, they are actually introducing stricter policies on immigration, integration, and terrorism themselves.

And the relevance of the far right is no longer limited to Europe either, if it ever was. A democratically elected far-right leader currently governs three of the five biggest countries in the world. In the case of Jair Bolsonaro in Brazil and Donald Trump in the US, they came to power on the list of non-far-right parties. In India, Prime Minister Narendra Modi is the leader of the BJP, the party representative of the well-established and -organized Hindutva movement, which includes violent, extremist groups like the National Volunteer Organization (RSS), of which Modi has been a member since he was eight years old. And in Israel, long-term prime minister Benjamin Netanyahu has brought his right-wing Likud party more and more in line with his various far-right coalition partners.

Was the Tea Party movement a populist radical right movement or a mainstream right-wing movement with populist radical right groups and individuals? Is the Republican Party in the US (still) a mainstream right-wing party with a far-right leader or has Trump successfully transformed the party in his image? Where does Britain's Conservative Party stop and the United Kingdom Independence Party (UKIP) or Brexit Party begin? Is there still a fundamental difference between Fidesz and the Movement for a Better Hungary (Jobbik), the original far-right party in Hungary, which in the past years has campaigned on a more moderate platform than the officially "conservative" Fidesz? The mainstreaming of the far right – in terms of ideology, politics, and organization – that characterizes the fourth wave has made the borders between the radical right and the mainstream right – and in some case left, as in the Czech Republic and Denmark – more and more difficult to establish.

2

Ideology

When we think about the far right, we tend to think about ideological features like antisemitism and racism, as well as political issues like immigration and security. Although the far-right movement is highly diverse, even within the two major subgroups, extreme right and radical right, there are many ideological features and political issues that are shared across groups and parties. This chapter first discusses the key ideologies within the extreme right, that is, fascism and Nazism, and the key ideological features of the (populist) radical right, that is, nativism, authoritarianism, and populism.[1] It then discusses how these ideological features play out in the major issues of the far right of the fourth wave: immigration, security, corruption, and foreign policy. Its views on gender will be discussed in chapter 9.

Ideology

Extreme right ideologies believe that inequalities are natural and outside of the purview of the state. They celebrate difference and hierarchy, and their core feature is elitism, which holds that some groups and individuals are superior to others and should therefore have more power. There are many different extreme right groups and ideas, which often disagree more than they agree. For example, absolutist monarchists and racists agree that the basis of power is blood, but the former refer exclusively to royal lineage, the latter to alleged racial differences. Some theocrats believe that the highest power comes from a "Holy Book," like the Bible or the Talmud, while fascists position it in the person of the leader. In this book, I focus exclusively on far-right groups that base their identity primarily on ethnic or racial categories, which means that those groups that are primarily monarchist or religious, and for which ethnic and racial distinctions are secondary or irrelevant, are not discussed.

The most important extreme right ideology is fascism, a syncretic ideology which draws on various left- and right-wing anti-democratic traditions. Historical Italian fascism, often referred to as Fascism with a capital "F," held that ultimate power rested in the leader, who was the embodiment of the nation and state. For fascists, the state is not just a legal institution, it is an ethical, organic, and spiritual entity which requires full loyalty and submission. In essence, fascism is totalitarian, in that it wants full control of society. Every aspect of life is to be controlled by the party/state and there is absolutely no space for independence. Unsurprisingly, fascism rejects democracy. Hitler stated that "democracy is the foul and filthy avenue to communism," while Mussolini rejected it as "electoralism."

Instead, fascism offers a "Third Way," which goes beyond liberalism and socialism. This is reflected in its economic doctrine of corporatism, in which society is organized in corporate groups, such as those of agriculture and the military, which are meant to work together, in an organic manner, to the benefit of the state. Fascism wants to realize a national "rebirth" and create a "new man," physically fit and ideologically pure, unbound by old hierarchies of class and heritage. As an ideology, fascism also believes in actions over words as well as war over peace. It believes that violence is power, and war not only is the natural state of life, but also purifies and regenerates the nation and state.

German fascism, better known as National Socialism or Nazism, shares many core features with (Italian) Fascism, but is more explicitly and fundamentally antisemitic and racist. Whereas fascists see the main entity as the state, a legal category, Nazis see it as the race, a supposedly biological category. Nazis believe that there are several different races and that the Aryan race is superior to all others. It is the right of the superior *Übermenschen* (superhumans) to dominate, and even exterminate, the inferior *Untermenschen* (subhumans). In the Nazis' worldview, Jews are seen as both morally and physically inferior, yet economically and politically powerful. Nazis claim that the actions and ideas – and especially "conspiracies" – of "the Jews" infect the Aryan race with moral and racial disease – hence their portrayal as rats (i.e. vermin) in propaganda such as the infamous 1940 movie *Der Ewige Jude* (*The Eternal Jew*).

It is important to situate the racism of the Nazis in its historical context. In the early twentieth century, antisemitism and racism were broadly accepted within German, and European, societies and even within parts of the scientific community. After the horrors of the Second World War, racism became largely unacceptable, and in some countries even illegal, while the whole concept of "race," and the existence of different "races," was mostly rejected. Instead, ingroups were increasingly defined in non-biological terms, most notably "ethnic groups" or "nations," which are both primarily cultural categories. A group of mainly French radical right activists, commonly known as the *nouvelle droite* (see chapter 3), developed a new ideology, which they termed *ethnopluralism*. Dismissed by opponents as merely "new racism," ethnopluralism argues that people are divided into ethnic groups, which are equal but should remain segregated. Whether implicitly or explicitly, ethnopluralism has become a core ideological feature of most relevant European radical right groups today.

That said, racism is not dead. It is still prominent within the extreme right (e.g. neo-Nazis and white supremacists) and even radical right politicians will at times slip into a racial or racist discourse. For instance, Martin Helme, the son of the leader of the Estonian Conservative People's Party (EKRE), and currently Estonian minister of finance, said on a Tallinn TV talk show, on recent riots and ethnic conflicts in Sweden, "Our immigration policy should have one simple rule: if you're black, go back." He also said, "I want Estonia to be a white country." Similarly, Thierry Baudet, leader of the new Dutch party Forum for Democracy (FvD), said in a discussion on the "refugee crisis" in 2015, "I don't want Europe to Africanize" and "I would really like Europe to stay dominantly white and culturally as it is now."

Whether informed primarily by racism or ethnopluralism, one of the key ideological features of the far right, and the dominant feature of the contemporary populist radical right, is *nativism*, a combination of nationalism and xenophobia. It is an ideology that holds that states should be inhabited exclusively by members of the native group (the nation) and that non-native (or "alien") elements, whether persons or ideas, are fundamentally threatening to the homogeneous nation-state. The core idea of nativism is best summarized in the slogan "Germany for the Germans, Foreigners Out," which became infamous as a rallying cry at the often-violent anti-refugee rallies of the early 1990s.

The ultimate goal of the populist radical right is an *ethnocracy*, that is, a democracy in which citizenship is based on ethnicity. It wants to (re)create this monocultural state by closing the borders to immigrants and giving "aliens" a choice between assimilation or repatriation. Those who are unwilling to assimilate, that is, become "native," must be expelled to the country they (or their ancestors) came from. However, populist radical right groups disagree about the scope of assimilation. Some believe that only "related" ethnic groups can assimilate – for example, only other (white) Europeans can become German or Hungarian – while others mainly hold that Islam is incompatible with their nation, meaning that Muslims cannot assimilate into "western" societies.

Within nativism, antisemitism and Islamophobia play particularly important roles. *Antisemitism*, hostility to or prejudice against Jews, was the key prejudice of the far right in the early twentieth century, and remains central to many extreme right groups today. However, many populist radical right groups and parties, particularly in Western Europe, are not antisemitic and some have even become philosemitic (pro-Jewish), seeing Israel as the ideal ethnocracy and Jews as natural allies in the struggle against Islam. *Islamophobia*, an irrational fear of Islam or Muslims, has become the defining prejudice of the far right of the fourth wave. In this view, Islam is equated with Islamism, that is, an extremist political interpretation of Islam, and Muslims are seen as hostile to democracy and to all non-Muslims – Islamophobes often proudly declare themselves to be "kuffars" or "infidels."

The term *authoritarianism* is often used to describe non-democratic leaders or political systems, but I use it

Islamophobic anti-Obama protester at Tea Party rally in Mishawaka, Indiana, in 2009. (Photo by author.)

in different manner, in line with a long tradition in social psychology. Here, authoritarianism refers to the belief in a strictly ordered society, in which infringements on authority are to be punished severely. Authoritarians see almost all "problems," including drug addiction or perceived sexual deviancy, as essentially law-and-order issues which can only be countered by a tough punitive approach and prevented by reintroducing "moral" or "traditional" education in schools.

Populism, finally, is the buzzword of the twenty-first century, but that prominence is in part a consequence of its conceptual confusion. I define populism as a (thin) ideology that considers society to be ultimately separated into two homogeneous and antagonistic groups, the pure people and the corrupt elite, and which argues that politics should be an expression of the *volonté générale* (general will) of the people. In essence, populists claim that the mainstream parties are working together to keep the people, of which the populists are the voice (i.e. the *vox populi*), from power. Indian prime minister and BJP leader Narendra Modi gave a good example in a speech in April 2018 when he declared that the Congress Party is for the elite (*namdaar*), whereas the BJP is for the people (*kaamdaars*).

In short, the far right consists, broadly, of two groups, the extreme right and the radical right, which hold fundamentally different positions on democracy. Whereas the extreme right rejects the essence of democracy – the idea of political equality and government by popular majority – the (populist) radical right supports democracy, at least in theory, but fundamentally challenges key institutions and values of liberal democracy, including minority rights, rule of law, and separation of powers. Hence, the difference between the two is not merely quantitative – in the sense that the extreme right is a more radical/extreme form of the radical right – it is also qualitative.

The different far-right groups and parties are acutely aware of this and often amplify their internal differences to sell themselves to potential followers. In general, extreme right groups attack radical right parties as corrupt and weak, "bourgeois" sellouts to the political establishment, who value acceptance by the political establishment, as well as individual material spoils, over their ideals. For their part, radical right parties denounce extreme right groups as full of crazies who are politically ineffective and/or dangerously violent. Many far-right groups spend more time denouncing their far-right "competitors" than their "real" enemies within the political establishment.

Rarely do they present each other as two sides of the same struggle. In fact, both accuse the other of undermining its righteous struggle. The radical right argues that the extreme right, through its ideological extremity and violent actions, discredits the broader struggle, while the extreme right holds that the radical right, because it works within the system, compromises the essence of the struggle, settling on compromises that uphold the fundaments of the despised political system.

Themes

During the third wave, the far right was often portrayed as a single-issue movement, exclusively concerned with immigration. This is incorrect. Immigration remains the key political issue for most far-right groups, particularly in Western Europe and North America, but it is only one of several issues that they campaign on. While there are many ideological and national variations, four political issue clusters are central to all far-right groups and parties around the globe: immigration, security, corruption, and foreign policy.

Immigration

The immigration issue includes two separate but related issues: immigration and integration. Immigration proper has long been one of the core issues of almost every far-right group in Europe and North America, but occasionally also features prominently in some countries in other regions (such as Brazil and Japan). Populist radical right parties typically claim that "mass immigration" constitutes an existential threat to their nation and state, while extreme right groups are more concerned about race, claiming that western countries are facing a "white genocide" because of mass immigration and state-sponsored multiculturalism.

In the twenty-first century, the conspiracy theory of "The Great Replacement" is at the heart of much of the anti-immigration rhetoric of the populist radical right – and, increasingly, the mainstream right. Popularized by French writers Jean Raspail and Renaud Camus, but building upon an antisemitic and racist tradition dating back to the late nineteenth century, the thesis holds that "the West" is being overrun by a "tidal wave" of non-Western immigration. Populist radical right politicians believe that mass immigration is not driven by poverty in developing countries, but organized by progressive politicians in the developed countries, who either hate their own nation or try to compensate for their lost electorate – which partly went to the populist radical right – by "importing" new voters. In recent years, strongly pushed by Hungarian premier Viktor Orbán, the Jewish US-Hungarian billionaire philanthropist George Soros has been seen as the evil genius in this conspiracy, reflecting a modern-day version of the infamous antisemitic classic *The Protocols of the Elders of Zion*.

Obviously, both "native" and "alien" are subjective terms. In the view of the far right, one is not simply native because one has citizenship of a country. In fact, many of the so-called "aliens" are born and bred in the "native" country, despite being falsely referred to as "immigrants" (not just by the far right). The key far-right "Other" of the twenty-first century is "the

Muslim," not just in Europe, but also in India and Israel as well as among many new groups in North America. Far from being exclusive to the far right, Islamophobia, and specifically a fear of "Islamization," dominates far-right propaganda, in which domestic and foreign developments are combined with conspiracy theories based on dubious statistics or simplistic narratives.

While many populist radical right politicians try to express their nativism in the largely neutral terms of ethnopluralism, they almost always argue or imply that the "native" culture is superior to the "alien" one(s). The far right describes "aliens" almost exclusively in derogatory terms. For example, BJP president Amit Shah claimed that Bangladeshi immigrants in India are "infiltrators" and "termites," Jewish Home leader, and then Israeli minister of education, Naftali Bennett referred to asylum seekers as "illegal infiltrators," and Brazilian president Jair Bolsonaro has called (Venezuelan) immigrants "scum of the earth."

Security

Far-right groups are obsessed with "security," but they interpret the concept much more broadly than just the physical security of individuals. Security refers both to individuals and to collectives, most notably the nation or race, and has a cultural, economic, and physical component. Almost every political issue is perceived through the lens of a "threat to the natural order," creating insecurity, which has to be dealt with by an iron hand. Whether it is drugs, immigration, or unemployment, the solution is found in authoritarian policies, celebrating the stick and criticizing the carrot. However, security almost always has a nativist component to it, given that "aliens" are seen as the key source of natives' insecurity.

Take the issue of crime, one of the most prominent themes in their propaganda. For the far right, crime is first and foremost an "alien" issue, in the sense that it almost exclusively focuses on (alleged) crimes committed by "non-natives." A striking example of this nativist fixation on crime is the Victims of Immigration Crime Engagement Office, an agency President Trump created within the Department of Homeland Security – itself an illustration of the securitization of immigration that followed the terrorist attacks of 9/11 in most western countries. Much far-right propaganda mentions "aliens" almost only as criminals and the few "native" crimes that are acknowledged are predominantly corruption cases by "progressive" political elites (see below).

According to the far right, crime is rampant, and increasing because of immigration and the "naïve" and "weak" policies of established politicians. Its propaganda is filled with selective and suggestive stories about "immigrant crime," or, in racial terms, "black-on-white crime," mostly from tabloids and right-wing media, which it presents as just the tip of the iceberg. When confronted with data that show that crime levels are actually decreasing, and are relatively low, as is the case in many western democracies, it tends to dismiss them as lies (e.g. Donald Trump's "fake news") produced by "the corrupt elite" and their "politically correct" minions to cover up the failures of multicultural society.

Key to the far right's programs around the globe are tough law and order issues, which it often shares with other right-wing groups, most notably conservatives. For the far right, crime is not related to socio-economic conditions – except if committed by poor "natives" – and has to be confronted with ruthless law enforcement. It therefore calls for more police on the streets and tougher sentences – but is divided on the death penalty – as well as less "political meddling" in law enforcement. Many groups also emphasize the need for schools to return to teaching youths discipline, respect, and "traditional values," notably the importance of the heterosexual family.

They link the issue of security to both elites (populism) and minorities (nativism). The youth are supposedly "indoctrinated" by left-wing teachers and academics who corrupt their innocent minds with "cultural Marxism" and other "perverse" ideas (see below). And it is because of the corruption or weakness of mainstream politicians that crime is rampant, and people feel insecure. For example, in India in 2018, Modi attacked the local Congress party in the state of Karnataka for interfering with the Lokayukta, an anti-corruption ombudsman organization, linking this directly to security: "In Karnataka there is no law, there is no order. The Lokayukta is not safe, how can the common people be safe." Similarly, in Brazil, during his 2018 presidential campaign, Bolsonaro proclaimed in one interview: "If a police officer kills ten, fifteen, or twenty alleged criminals with ten or thirty bullets each, he needs to get a medal and not be prosecuted."

However, the only way to truly stop the rise of crime, according to the far right, is to stop immigration. After all, in its world, crime is an almost exclusively "alien" phenomenon. Hence, Trump and other US nativists emphasize the crucial importance of building a wall on the southern border with Mexico – implying, against empirical evidence, that most crime in the US is committed by Latin American immigrants – while in the Netherlands Geert Wilders of the PVV campaigned from 2010 with the slogan "more security, less immigration." The most powerful, and racist, visualization of this mix of authoritarianism and nativism is the infamous campaign poster of the SVP in which a group of white sheep kick a black sheep off the Swiss flag under the slogan "creating security."

While the interrelation between crime and immigration has been a staple of the far right since at least the 1980s, the connection to the issue of terrorism is a more recent phenomenon. In the post-9/11 world, terrorism and Islam have been closely linked, in both mainstream and far-right discourse. Far-right groups rarely use the term "terrorism" for anything else than Islamist political violence, often minimizing, if not outright defending, "anti-immigrant" violence – or far-right-inspired violence against other groups, including representatives of left-wing groups and the state. For the far right, terrorism is closely related to immigration and multiculturalism. France's Marine Le Pen even went so far in 2017 as to call multiculturalism a weapon for Islamic extremists and claim that (multicultural) France has become "a university for Jihadists."

Corruption

While far-right propaganda primarily targets ethnic and racial "Others," internal and external to the country, the issue of corruption is almost exclusively linked to people from the in-group. Corruption is often mixed with authoritarianism, nativism, and, particularly, populism. It is a particular "elite" who are connected to corruption. On the one hand, it is the powerful, notably mainstream politicians, but also often economic elites, who are accused of stealing from the people. On the other hand, it is a political elite, broadly described as "the left," who are accused of corrupting the nation with "postmodernist" and "cultural Marxist" ideas – both terms, but particularly the latter, having strong antisemitic overtones. As Britain's UKIP tweeted in December 2018, "Make no mistakes, the EU wants to control your thoughts through your speech to spread its Postmodernist Neo-Marxist ideology."

Of course, in many countries, financial corruption by economic and political elites is a real and serious issue. For example, Bulgarian or Italian populist radical right parties don't have to invent scandals as their countries have long been plagued by widespread corruption. At the same time, even in these countries, many politicians are not corrupt – while several populist radical right parties (e.g. LN and RN) and politicians (e.g. Bolsonaro and Trump) have been linked to corruption too. But even in countries that are broadly acknowledged as not corrupt, like Estonia or Sweden, populist radical right parties use almost identical accusations. Far-right groups also argue that "the elite" corrupt the political system by electoral fraud. For example, both BJP president Shah and US president Trump have pushed the unsubstantiated claim that millions of "illegal immigrants" have been voting in elections in their respective countries.

Elites are also charged with corrupting the minds of the people, particularly of women (see chapter 9) and the youth. Far-right politicians from across the globe have accused academics, artists, and journalists not just of being elitist or left-wing, but also of being "anti-national": that is, traitors of the nation, the worst insult for a nationalist. For instance, Jewish Home politicians regularly attack progressive civil society organizations like the New Israel Fund, while the BJP has harassed domestic and foreign NGOs, including the Ford Foundation and Greenpeace, and has accused left-wing professors of having "occupied" academia and turned the youth against the nation. Extreme right politicians tend to substitute nation for race, but make similar claims, although they have a particular obsession with "race-mixing," which they consider a form of genocide. A special role in "white genocide" conspiracy theories is almost always reserved for "the Jews," who are alleged to mastermind all such plots in order to submit the white race to their power.

Foreign Policy

The far right lives in a dog-eat-dog world in which international relations are a zero-sum game: everyone is out for their own success, and so when one wins, the others lose. This is not to say it opposes any international cooperation, or does not care about other countries (or nations), but rather that this is always at best secondary to national (or racial) concerns – hence, Trump's "America First" policy has many national variants. Moreover, far-right groups have always been very suspicious of, and mostly outright hostile to, supranational organizations, from the strong EU to the much weaker United Nations (UN). But as much as they criticize the existing world order, they don't really have clear alternative visions, let alone one unified vision.

Irredentism, or the claim on some "lost" territory, plays a major role in the political program of many far-right groups, particularly in Central and Eastern Europe, where borders have shifted repeatedly in the past century. For instance, with the 1920 Treaty of Trianon, Hungary lost almost two-thirds of its territory – something that all the country's far-right organizations are obsessed with reversing. From Fidesz to the 64 Counties Youth Movement, they claim to represent all "ethnic Hungarians" – including the millions of Hungarian speakers in Romania, Serbia, Slovakia, and Ukraine – and strive to reunite all Hungarian territories.

Similarly, the struggle for Greater Israel (*Eretz Yisrael*) is at the heart of almost all Israeli far-right groups, while far-right organizations in India and Japan are focused on border disputes with Pakistan and China, respectively. The far right in Russia has a particularly dazzling myriad of irredentist fantasies, from a Eurasian Empire to a renewed Soviet Union under (explicit) Russian leadership. The most extreme is that of Vladimir Zhirinovsky, the longest-serving leader of a major far-right party in the world, the terribly misnamed Liberal Democratic Party of Russia. He once stated that he dreams of a time "when Russian soldiers can wash their boots in the warm waters of the Indian Ocean."

A second obsession of most far-right groups is supranational organizations, which are seen as a first step towards (cosmopolitan) one-world government. While most far-right groups are not fond of the UN, almost only US groups make a big issue out of this largely toothless organization. Conspiracy theories about secret plans to invade and occupy the US – ranging from Agenda 21 to black helicopters – reach deep inside the conservative movement, while far-right groups see the dawn of a "New World Order," after former President George H.W. Bush's famous "slip of the tongue" in a 1992 speech. Israeli far-right groups consider the UN to be an antisemitic organization, dominated by Arab states, and intent on destroying the State of Israel. And in his maiden speech to the Australian parliament in 2016, Australian ONP senator Malcolm Roberts called upon his country to leave the "socialistic, monolithic" UN.

Unsurprisingly, the actually powerful EU is a major concern for the European far right, which considers it a threat to national sovereignty. As Euroscepticism started to spread among European publics in the wake of the 1992 Maastricht Treaty, most far-right groups and parties became more outspoken and radical in their opposition to the EU. This has only increased after the so-called "refugee crisis" of 2015, as German chancellor Angela Merkel's pro-refugee policy and the EU's (ultimately unsuccessful) refugee redistribution plan infuriated the far right. This sentiment is clearly expressed in a 2018 tweet by Santiago Abascal, the leader of the newest stars in the European populist radical right firmament, the Spanish party Vox, who ranted against "the globalist oligarchy, freeloading on [public] budgets, which hopes to impose failed models on the people, [and] now dedicates itself to demonizing democracy and the sovereignty of nations."

During the third wave, most populist radical right parties were on the defensive with respect to European integration. Only a few openly called for their country to exit the EU, but almost all parties believed that the integration process had gone too far, particularly after the signing of the Maastricht Treaty, and wanted to roll back newer initiatives and stop further integration. The EU was seen as a hostile and remote bureaucracy in which "nationalist" forces had no voice. As a consequence of their growing electoral successes and political relevance in the fourth wave, populist radical right parties have become more ambitious and bold with regard to the EU. This is particularly true for populist radical right leaders in Central and Eastern Europe, who see their own countries as the "bulwark of Christianity" (PiS leader Jarosław Kaczynskí in Poland) and "the future of Europe" (Fidesz leader Viktor Orbán in Hungary).

Today, few relevant populist radical right parties still want to leave the EU. Both Marine Le Pen and Geert Wilders had shifted to an exit position in 2013, only to muddle it later on – partly due to the European backlash to the incompetent handling of Brexit by the British government. Most populist radical right parties remain Eurosceptic, however, wanting to "reform" the EU into a looser and more democratic organization which returns national sovereignty to its member states. Still, they differ on the fundamental nature of the future Europe. Ethnic nationalist parties like the Belgian VB want a "Europe of Nations," but state nationalist parties like France's RN and Spain's Vox prefer a "Europe of Fatherlands" (i.e. current states), fearing separatism at home. And while Fidesz and PiS call for a "Christian Europe," most West European populist radical right parties are much less comfortable with a continent defined in explicitly religious terms.

Finally, far-right parties are deeply divided on how the world should be ordered. During the Cold War, many radical right parties, somewhat grudgingly, supported the western NATO alliance, while most extreme right groups proposed a post-fascist Third Way. Today, many are worried about a unipolar world dominated by the US, even under President Trump, and embrace a stronger Russia to counter US hegemony. True to visions of French grandeur, Marine Le Pen has proposed a nationalist Washington–Paris–Moscow axis between her, Trump, and Putin. But many East European far-right groups, like EKRE and PiS, are deeply Russophobic and prefer a US-dominated world. Similarly, in India Modi seems fairly supportive of a dominant US, for now, while in Brazil Bolsonaro has vowed to work with Trump, in particular to oppose China's growing power.

The Role of Religion

Far-right ideologies can be combined with all religions as well as with a non-religious and even anti-religious position. Italian Fascism was initially anti-religious, but shifted to a more non-religious position after coming to a pragmatic agreement with the Vatican. Most contemporary European populist radical right groups are at best culturally Christian, in the sense that they consider Christianity, or a specific denomination (e.g. Roman Catholicism), as part of the national culture. Some go even a step further, arguing that one specific religion is part of the nation. For example, the DF's program states that "the Danish Evangelical Lutheran Church is the Church of the Danish people," while SD leader Jimmie Åkesson has said that the Church of Sweden should be reinstated as a state church. In light of the rising importance of Islamophobia, many populist radical right parties have become more outwardly Christian, embracing Christianity or more vaguely "Judeo-Christian values," without becoming truly religious parties. For instance, the Austrian FPÖ, which was founded as an anti-clerical party, has recently become a staunch defender of orthodox Catholics like former St. Pölten bishop Kurt Krenn, a vocal opponent of Islam and Muslim immigration.

The link between the far right and Christianity is strong in the US, at least on the populist radical right. Politicians from Pat Buchanan to Sarah Palin have defined the US as a "Christian nation" and have emphasized the importance of Christianity to politics. On the extreme right, the KKK has always been deeply religious, changing from exclusively Protestant to inclusively Christian over time (see vignette 1). However, many extreme right groups are only nominally Christian, or even explicitly anti-Christian, arguing that Christianity is "Jewish." For instance, groups like the now almost defunct Aryan Nations adhere to Christian Identity, an antisemitic and racist form of "Christianity," in which whites are the true "Chosen People" and all non-whites are seen as soulless "mud people."

Outside of the US, some far-right groups and politicians are openly Christian in a religious way. Bolsonaro ran with the initial slogan "Brazil above everything, and God above us all." The Polish PiS is deeply Catholic and closely associated with the most nationalist and orthodox elements of the Polish Catholic Church. It has argued that the "European Constitution" should include a reference to "God," and has made its orthodox interpretation of Catholicism a leading principle in many of its education, family, and health policies. The small neo-fascist New Force in Italy is fundamentalist Catholic and strives for the "recovery of Christian religiosity" and "faith in the Catholic Church."

In general, ties between the far right and religion are closer in Orthodox Christian countries, from Greece to Russia, given that most Orthodox Churches are national churches and have strong nationalist traditions. In Romania, small neo-Guardist groups remain loyal to an esoteric combination of mysticism and Orthodoxy – a faith which in the early twentieth century defined the original Legion of the Archangel Michael, more popularly known as the Iron Guard. In Ukraine, several far-right groups, like Svoboda and C14, support the schismatic Orthodox Church of Ukraine, which split from the official Ukrainian Orthodox Church, an autonomous branch of the Russian Orthodox Church, in 2018.

In contrast, there are quite strong pagan, and explicitly anti-Christian, strands within the European far right too. The French *nouvelle droite* is officially pagan, arguing that "Judeo-Christian monotheism" has become secularized. Following the German philosopher Friedrich Nietzsche, its main thinker, Alain De Benoist, argued in his book *On Being a Pagan* (1981) that Christianity must be destroyed, and a new "Indo-European" paganism should be created. Various extreme right groups also hark back to (alleged) pre-Christian beliefs, including various forms of *Ásatrú* (heathenry). In the late twentieth century, Odinism, and particularly its racial form, Wotanism, which worships Nordic gods like Odin and Thor, became popular among some neo-Nazi groups. Elements of Wotanism can also be found in some Christian Identity groups, as well as the now practically defunct "Creativity" movement, while some extreme right groups even practice Satanism.

Hindutva ideology is perhaps the most perfect mix of nativism and religion. Going back to the classic text *Essentials of Hindutva* (1923) by Vinayak Damodar Savarkar, it replaces purely religious Hinduism with more nationalist *Hindu Rashtra*, that is, the Hindu nation. Initially, it also had a strong racist component, referring to the *Arya* (Hindu race), as Savarkar was strongly influenced by European fascism, particularly Nazism. While contemporary Hindutva groups like the BJP and RSS no longer (openly) support fascism or biological racism, they remain committed to a staunchly xenophobic Hindu nationalism. With the exception of some specific groups that are seen as part of the Hindu fraternity (e.g. Buddhists and Sikhs), Hindutva groups consider non-Hindus like Christians and Muslims as threats to the Hindu nation and an obstacle to the desired Hindu state (Hindustan).

Buddhism has long been seen as an exceptional religion, untainted by religious fanatics or violent nationalists. This image was shattered by recent events in Myanmar. While the government and military mostly justify the brutal repression of the Muslim Rohingya in terms of national security, far-right groups like the decentralized 969 Movement and the Organization for the Protection of Race and Religion, as well as extremist leaders like monk Ashin Wirathu, want to punish everyone who "insults" Buddhism. This includes, by definition, people of other religions. Far-right Buddhists have not only been involved in violent pogroms against the Rohingya minority, but have also branded Myanmar human rights groups as "traitors on national affairs" and accused them of being backed by foreign groups.

Unsurprisingly, the connection with religion is very strong among the Jewish far right, given their ethno-religious definition of the nation. With few exceptions

– notably Israel Our Home, which caters primarily to secular Russian immigrants – Israeli far-right groups combine ethnic nationalism with religious Judaism. The National Religious camp, mainly represented by Jewish Home and its most recent split, New Right, has long based its struggle for the annexation of "Judea and Samaria" (the West Bank) on the biblical argument that God gave the Land of Israel to its Chosen People (the Jews). The most extreme fusion of Israeli nationalism and Jewish religion is Kahanism, which combines fascism with religious fundamentalism. According to the late Rabbi Meir Kahane, not only should Israel occupy the whole "Land of Israel," but also only (real) Jews should inhabit it, and all non-Jews should be (forcefully) expelled.

One of the few clear examples of a far-right Muslim movement, at least in the essentially nativist sense defined here, is the Turkish Nationalist Action Party (MHP). Initially a secularist party, it embraced Islam in the 1970s, arguing "We are as Turk as the Tengri mountain and as Muslim as the Hira mountain. Both philosophies are our principles." In the 1980s, the Idealist faction broke off and founded the Grand Unity Party, which combines Turkish nationalism with Islamism. Islam plays a central role in Malay nationalism too. While the former ruling United Malays National Organization combines Malay nationalism with a multinational society, albeit with decades of racial politics, it is increasingly struggling with more radical Malay nationalists, who believe only Muslims can be real Malays, and who attack non-Muslims (notably Chinese, Christians, and Hindus).

Vignette 1: Shifting "Us" and "Them"

All far-right ideologies are built around a strict us-versus-them opposition, but both the *us* and the *them* can change over time. As groups have come to consider different "Others" as threatening, they have changed not only the "them," but also the "us." This is the case not just across different groups, but even within similar groups.

A good example of these shifting identities is the KKK, which wreaked havoc in the US South in the late 1860s. Founded by former Confederate soldiers, the Klan claimed to defend the White Anglo-Saxon Protestant (WASP) Southerner and targeted both African Americans and Yankees in the South (derogatively referred to as "carpet-baggers"), although they primarily killed the former. The second KKK, which emerged in the early twentieth century, was not merely a Southern phenomenon. No longer opposing Yankees, it was particularly successful above the Mason–Dixon line, including in Indiana and Illinois. Still hating African Americans (and Jews), the new Klan now mainly railed against Catholic immigration from Europe. The third and current iteration of the KKK, a mostly Southern reaction to the civil rights movement of the 1960s, is still deeply antisemitic and racist, but primarily defends "Christian whites" instead of only WASPs. They increasingly overlap with neo-Nazi groups, which have replaced the Nazis' "Aryan" race with the broader "white" race, thereby no longer excluding Slavs and other non-Germanic whites.

A more recent transformation of us and them identities can be seen in the fourth wave, in which the main enemies of the populist radical right have become Islam and Muslims. While it defined "immigrants" primarily in ethno-national terms in the 1980s and 1990s, the largely similar "aliens" are mainly described in ethno-religious terms today – an important, legal, difference is that most of the former were indeed immigrants, whereas most "aliens" today are actually citizens, born and raised in Western Europe or the US. In the post-9/11 world, and the ongoing "War on Terror," Turks and Moroccans in Germany and the Netherlands, or Bengalis and Pakistanis in the UK, have become (just) Muslims. Unsurprisingly, this has led many far-right groups to emphasize or even rediscover their own religious roots, redefining the "us" more in terms of Christian or "Judeo-Christian civilization."

But the "us" can even change in national terms. The FPÖ was founded in the 1950s as a Great German party, defining Austrians as part of the German nation, and rejecting the construct of an Austrian nation as an "ideological monstrosity." But in the 1980s, in its attempt to increase electoral support, the FPÖ shed its Great German ideology and redefined itself as the party of "Austrian patriots." Similarly, Umberto Bossi founded the LN in staunch opposition to the Italian state. The party later even invented its own nation, Padania, with a new currency, flag, and passport. But when Matteo Salvini took over in 2013, he rebuilt the moribund LN as an Italian party, downplaying regionalism (and Padania) as well as attacks on Southern Italians, and prioritizing attacks on Muslims and, more recently, refugees. Salvini even dropped "Nord" from the party name, successfully campaigning as Lega (League) with the slogan "Italians first" in the 2018 parliamentary elections.

3

Organization

Far-right politics comes in a broad variety of forms, not just in terms of ideology and issues, but also in types of organizations. Some groups have millions of supporters, others just a handful. Some are purely intellectual, others primarily violent. Some are, organizationally speaking, more similar to mainstream political parties like Britain's Conservative Party or Labour Party, others to US criminal gangs like the Bloods and the Crips.

There are many different ways to slice up the far right organizationally, and none of them is perfect. I roughly follow the distinction introduced by the German political scientist Michael Minkenberg,[1] although with slightly different terminology, distinguishing between political parties, social movement organizations, and subcultures. Simply stated, political parties run for elections, social movement organizations do not, and while parties and social movement organizations are reasonably well-organized groups, subcultures are not.

In the following sections, I describe the main characteristics and representatives of the different organizational structures within the contemporary far right. It is not an attempt to be exhaustive, and by the time you read this, some might already be dated. Many far-right organizations are still very fluid and temporal; they come and go and sometimes even change roles (e.g. from party to social movement organization). The chapter ends with a discussion of the international collaboration of the far right, a topic of grandiose speculation, but whose reality is much more modest.

Political Parties

In their most essential form, political parties are political groups that contest elections to public office. Given that most democracies are party democracies, in which almost all crucial political positions are occupied by people elected on a party ticket, far-right political parties are at the core of the fourth wave. They contest elections in the vast majority of western democracies, and are getting elected to a majority of their national parliaments. At the same time, far-right parties differ in many ways. Leaving aside ideological differences, which have been addressed previously, far-right parties differ in terms of organizational structure, often but not always a consequence of their respective age. The two extremes are the Indian BJP, which resembles the mass party of the mid-twentieth century, and the Dutch PVV, which literally is a one-man party.

Founded in 1980, the BJP is the main party-political representative of the *Sangh Parivar* (Family of Organizations), the broader Hindu nationalist (*Hindutva*) movement that organizes and represents tens of millions of people across the globe. The BJP has dominated two right-wing coalition governments in India and currently controls many of the country's most populous and important states. It claims to have almost

BJP supporters riding motorbikes carrying BJP flags in New Delhi, India, after winning the 2014 parliamentary election. (Source: Arindam Banerjee/Dreamstime.com/2014.)

one hundred million members, which would make it the biggest political party in the world – even bigger than the Chinese Communist Party. It is a cadre-based party that draws its leadership from the party and the broader *Sangh Parivar*, while its members are organized in hundreds of local, regional, and state branches, including a host of auxiliary organizations, including for farmers, students, and workers, as well as for women, youth, and, interestingly, minorities. "Non-Resident Indians" and other BJP supporters residing outside of India are organized in the Overseas Friends of Bharatiya Janata Party, which claims branches in forty countries across all inhabited continents.

In sharp contrast, the PVV is the most extreme example of a leader-party, given that Geert Wilders is not just the leader of the party, he literally *is* the party. Wilders was a rising backbencher for the conservative People's Party for Freedom and Democracy in the Netherlands who faced pushback for his increasingly strident opposition to Islam and Turkish EU membership. In 2005, he split from the party, continuing for the rest of the legislative period as Group Wilders, before founding the PVV the next year. The party has only two statutory members, Wilders and a foundation of which he is the only member.

All other far-right parties fall somewhere in between these two extremes, with modest levels of membership and organization, and a relatively small cadre of party activists who are almost independent from the party membership. Many parties are dependent upon state funding, which is linked to electoral results and/or parliamentary seats, explaining why few far-right parties survive outside of parliament. In most cases, when they cannot get a foothold in parliament, they remain parties in name only, functioning mainly as political organizations, which rarely contest elections, and never with significant success.

Compared to most mainstream political parties – be they left, right, or center – far-right parties have an organizational structure that is more centralized and leader-centric. Such a structure is not uncommon for new parties, but far-right parties rarely truly democratize. Some hold elections for the party leader among their members, but they are "guided" at best, with the leadership strictly controlling the election procedures and vetting "suitable" candidates from an in-crowd of party cadres. This often leads to frustration and rebellion, but also ensures a relatively smooth transfer of power with relatively marginal changes in ideology, organization, and personnel. Hence, contrary to the popular image of the "flash party," surviving for just one or two elections, several far-right parties have survived initial electoral defeats and internal struggles and are now successfully established within their respective political systems.

Social Movement Organizations

There are a myriad of far-right groups beyond political parties, which range from well-structured, well-funded organizations with hundreds of thousands of members to marginal groupuscules so tiny that they could fit in one bedroom. Many of these organizations are part of a larger social movement, to which they bring some level of structure and permanence. While all organizations share a far-right ideology, they have very different activities, agendas, and constituencies. I focus here primarily on intellectual, media, and political organizations.

Intellectual Organizations

The far right is not a particularly intellectual movement – in fact many far-right groups are openly anti-intellectual, considering all "intellectuals" to be "cultural Marxists" (see chapter 2). But there are some organizations that focus on developing and innovating far-right ideas and educating primarily far-right activists. This includes both specific organizations within the more successful political parties, which organize thematic conferences and summer schools to educate their cadres, and groups that focus exclusively on education, for example by publishing books and magazines.

The most important intellectual far-right movement is the *nouvelle droite* (New Right), a very loosely structured movement of individuals and magazines that spans the globe. These "Gramscians of the Right" believe a political victory can only follow cultural hegemony, which is to be achieved by actively changing the political discourse. They position themselves as anti-1968ers, being both inspired and triggered by the success of the New Left of that period. In many ways, the *nouvelle droite* has copied New Left strategies and tactics, albeit somewhat less successfully (for now).

Its origins lie in the Research and Study Group for European Civilization (GRECE), founded in 1968, whose major figure is Alain De Benoist. The *nouvelle droite* has been instrumental in modernizing classic far-right thinking by replacing classic racism, based on biology and superiority, with ethnopluralism, based on ethnicity and (alleged) equality. It argues that cultures are equal but different, and people can only fully flourish within their own culture, which it associates with a set of traditions. Consequently, it opposes multiculturalism, which it, paradoxically, considers racist. More recently, the Identitarian movement has taken the *nouvelle droite*'s ideas out of the boring constraints of magazines and think tanks and combined it with mediagenic street politics (see vignette 3 in chapter 5).

The US has a broad range of right-wing think tanks, some of which spread core beliefs of the far right. These include anti-immigration organizations like the Federation for Immigration Reform, and allied groups like the Center for Immigration Studies and Numbers USA, which have become fully mainstreamed under the Trump presidency. Similarly, Islamophobic organizations like Frank Gaffney's Center for Security Policy and National Security Advisor John Bolton's Gatestone Institute have become key players in the Trump administration, showing the partial overlap between radical right and (neo-)conservative ideologies and policies – notably in a shared Islamophobia and distrust, or even rejection, of multinational organizations like the UN. At the same time, so-called "alt right" organizations, like Jared Taylor's American Renaissance and Richard Spencer's National Policy Institute, have remained solidly excluded, even during the Trump presidency.

In recent years, far-right activists have also tried to establish their own educational initiatives. Many

European parties were already organizing "summer universities," particularly to educate and socialize their most promising members (their current and future cadres). For example, the FN has been organizing summer universities throughout France for decades, while the VB, and its youth wing, Flemish Interest Youth, has done the same, moving around Europe (including Austria, Croatia, France, and Spain). Most of these gatherings are more summer camp than university, particularly when organized for youth, with a host of physical activities combined with lectures by far-right speakers from inside and outside of the respective party.

More recently, Marion Maréchal-Le Pen, Marine Le Pen's niece, stepped back from active party politics within the FN to establish the Institute of Social Sciences, Economics, and Politics in Lyon. The goal of the new institute is to "detect and train the leaders of tomorrow who will have the courage, intelligence, discernment and competence to act effectively ... in the service of society." Earlier, in Poland, the far right, ultra-orthodox Catholic priest Tadeusz Rydzyk, who previously had supported the League of Polish Families (LPR) and is now close to PiS, founded the College of Social and Media Culture in Toruń in 2001. Its graduates have taken prominent places in the private and public Polish media, particularly when PiS is in power.

Media Organizations

The far right has always had its own media organizations, but most were part of larger, or simply better-financed, parties and movements. This applies both to newspapers like the *Deutsche National-Zeitung*, which was published by Dr. Gerhard Frey, the leader of the small German People's Union party, or *Éléments* and *Nouvelle École*, published by GRECE. Most of these publications had a relatively limited audience, reaching not much beyond the (dedicated) membership of their parent organizations.

During the fourth wave, many new far-right media organizations have emerged as a consequence of two developments: (1) the emergence of social media; and (2) the success and mainstreaming of the populist radical right. As soon as the Internet took shape in the 1990s, far-right entrepreneurs saw the advantages for the movement and established a significant presence. Among the first, and for a long time most important, was the *Stormfront* website, operated by ex-KKK leader Don Black, which functioned for many years as the hub for global neo-Nazis and white supremacists. The US far right is highly active online, including through websites like the radical right *Breitbart News*, the neo-Nazi *Daily Stormer*, the conspiratorial *Info Wars*, and the white supremacist *V-DARE*. In Canada, *Rebel Media* functions as an equivalent of *Breitbart News*, while *GeenStijl* (No Style) could be seen as a less professional Dutch equivalent (albeit, technically, a predecessor).

There are a host of European far-right online and offline media too, claiming to provide "real" or "uncensored" news, particularly on the far right's favorite issues like crime, corruption, European integration, and immigration. Some of the more prominent include the Czech *Parlementní Listy* (Parliamentary List), the German *Junge Freiheit* (Young Freedom), the Polish *Gazeta Polska* (Polish Newspaper), and the Spanish *Caso Aislado* (Isolated Case). Outside of Europe and North America, some key far-right media include *Arutz Sheva* (Israel National News) in Israel, *OPEN Magazine* in India, and the online web portal *R7* in Brazil.

Many of the primarily Islamophobic media websites, like *The Brussels Journal*, *Gates of Vienna*, and *Voice of Europe*, claim to be "conservative," which in part reflects the growing ideological and personal convergence between conservative and populist radical right subcultures on issues like immigration and Islam. This convergence, or transformation, has also made some established conservative media into voices of the populist radical right. In Hungary, almost all public and private media have come under the control of the radical right government, and now function as Viktor Orbán's propaganda instruments (see vignette 4 in chapter 7).

Political Organizations

Most far-right groups are political groups, or at least aspire to influence the politics of their country. In fact, some are fairly similar to political parties, in that they have a formal membership, an ideological program, and a fairly sophisticated organizational structure. What distinguishes them from political parties is that they don't contest elections – or have stopped doing so. But the borders are porous, as some political (and social) organizations will occasionally contest elections, at least in some localities, even if they mainly organize non-electoral activities (see chapter 5).

The bulk of far-right political organizations are marginal, with at best a few dozen activists and only a local or online presence. They perform mostly a social function, providing a (safe) meeting space for politically likeminded people, and rarely engage in public activities. This applies as much to the various *Kameradschaften* (Comraderies) in Germany as to the KKK in the US. Even slightly bigger organizations, like the now banned National Action in the UK and the National Socialist Movement in the US, organize only a few, badly attended, rallies, even if they can be responsible for serious violence.

But there are also much bigger and more powerful far-right political organizations, which influence party politics, sometimes even in countries without a strong far-right party. A good example is Japan Conference (Nippon Kaigi), founded in 1997, and with a membership of around 38,000 people, organized in some 230 local branches. Japan Conference is devoted to constitutional revision and historical revisionism, wanting to re-establish Japan as a military power and restore the country's (and emperor's) honor by "changing the postwar national consciousness," which is based on the "illegitimate" Tokyo War Crimes tribunals of 1946–8. While not a political party itself, it is a major player within the Liberal Democratic Party, Japan's dominant political party. A staggering fifteen of the eighteen members of the third Abe Cabinet (2014–18) were members of Japan Conference, including Prime Minister Shinzō Abe, while the organization also claimed 289 of the 480 members of the Japanese parliament.

In recent years, we have seen a few national, and even transnational, organizations that have been reasonably successful in street politics. The English Defence League (EDL) organized various Islamophobic rallies in England, which attracted at times thousands of protesters. Mixing far-right and hooligan cultures, the EDL quickly became a media sensation, leading to offshoots in Europe, North America, and Australasia. However, in recent years it has suffered from declining numbers of demonstrators and internal power struggles. Similarly, Patriotic Europeans Against the Islamization of the Occident (PEGIDA) took the media by storm, despite attracting a sizeable crowd only in Dresden, in the east of Germany, its city of origin. A somewhat similar group in Japan is the Association of Citizens Against the Special Privileges of *Zainichi*, the Korean minority in Japan. Better known as Zaitokukai, it was founded in 2007, and has a volatile, loosely defined and structured, membership that peaked at around 15,000.[2] While Zaitokukai is mostly active on the Internet, it has organized many, mainly smaller, demonstrations against the alleged privileges of the *Zainichi* as well as immigration and immigrants more generally.

Subcultures

Subcultures are groups within the larger national culture that share an identity, values, practices, and cultural objects. Within a subculture, people's common identity is based upon a perceived similar culture (including ideas and symbols) rather than an institutional affiliation. This is not to say that subcultures never include (strong) institutions. Examples of national far-right subcultures are the *Nemzeti Rock* (national rock) subculture in Hungary – which includes a large number of festivals, groups, and even radio stations – and the *Uyoku dantai* in Japan, a loose network of far-right groups that are particularly known for their *gaisensha*, that is, buses and vans covered in propaganda slogans and fitted with loudspeakers, which drive through the streets in small convoys.

There are very few truly far-right international subcultures. In most cases, the far right is part of a broader subculture, either as individuals or as a sub-subculture. Owing to the media obsession with the far right, it can come to define broader subcultures in the public imagination, even if it actually constitutes a (loud and violent) minority, as used to be the case with football hooligans and remains the case with skinheads. In the following section, I will discuss some of the more relevant and well-known far-right subcultures as well as some subcultures with a significant far-right presence.

"Alt-Right"

The so-called "alt-right," short for alternative right, is a somewhat unfortunate term which has gained popularity in the US and beyond in recent years. It was popularized by Richard Spencer, a well-educated white nationalist, with the aim of bringing together as broad a group of "race realists" as possible. Aware that ideologies and terms like white nationalism and white supremacy scared away many, particularly better-educated, people because of their negative connotations, Spencer used the term "alt-right," which broke out of its shadow as a consequence of the rise of Donald Trump and, in particular, Hillary Clinton's ill-advised "alt-right" speech of August 2016.

The essence of the "alt-right" is best captured by the Southern Poverty Law Center, a US anti-racist group, which described it as "a set of far-right ideologies, groups and individuals whose core belief is that 'white identity' is under attack by multicultural forces using 'political correctness' and 'social justice' to undermine white people and 'their' civilization."[3] As with all subcultures, there are only a handful of significant groups or organizations. One of the few organizations with some durability is Spencer's marginal National Policy Institute, a self-described "independent organization dedicated to the heritage, identity, and future of people of European descent in the United States and around the world."

What sets the "alt-right" apart from other far-right subcultures is that it is almost exclusively an online phenomenon. And even online it has a minimal organizational infrastructure. There are some online magazines, like *American Renaissance* (Jared Taylor), *Counter Currents* (Greg Johnson), and *Taki's Magazine* (named after founder Taki Theodoracopulos), but most alt-right activity is unorganized and anonymous and takes place on broader platforms like *4chan* and *Reddit*. It consists mostly of trolling people on social media, like Facebook and Twitter, by posting misogynist and racist memes or posts. There is a significant overlap with other amorphous online subcultures, most notably the gamer world and the so-called "manosphere" (see chapter 9), all dominated by younger, more educated, white males.

Emboldened by Donald Trump's election to the presidency in 2016, even though it has a complicated relationship to him, the "alt-right" tried to create an offline presence. The most successful event was the "Unite the Right" rally in Charlottesville, Virginia, in August 2017. It attracted roughly 1,000 people, although mostly from more traditional neo-Nazi and white supremacist groups like various Klans and the National Socialist Movement, and ended in violence and the murder of counter-protester Heather Heyer. Since then, "alt-right" rallies have rarely attracted more than a few dozen protesters, in addition to many more anti-fascists, and in March 2018 Spencer abandoned his intended university speaking tour after a few months, fed up with anti-fascist violence and legal battles with reluctant university administrators.

Today the "alt-right" remains a mostly anonymous online phenomenon. While international in scope, the subculture is very focused on the Anglo-Saxon world, most notably the US. Even bloggers and vloggers from other countries, like the Swedish–US couple Hendrik Palmgren and Lara Lokteff, of the website *Red Ice*, and Canadian Lauren Southern, formerly of *Rebel Media*, primarily address a US audience. This is even the case for the Swedish businessman Daniel Friberg, who has financed far-right projects in the US – including the website *AltRight.com*.

Football Hooligans

In terms of core demographics, far-right groups, football supporters, and street violence all disproportionately attract young, white, working-class males. The existence of far-right football hooligans is therefore not overly surprising, but its relevance has been significantly overplayed in alarmist media accounts and sensationalist hooligan literature. While much violence was more or less spontaneous, involving fluid groups of ever-changing football supporters, there were also more organized groups of hooligans, so-called "firms," which created a shadowy subculture and structure with their own codes and clothes. Among the most notorious British firms with a strong far-right presence were the Headhunters (Chelsea FC), the Inter City Firm (West Ham United), the Service Crew (Leeds United), and the Soul Crew (Cardiff City).

Far-right hooliganism migrated to the European continent in the 1980s, where local hooligans largely mimicked British firms. Some big European clubs with infamous far-right hooligans are/were Borussia Dortmund and Hansa Rostock (Germany), Hellas Verona and SS Lazio (Italy), FC Feyenoord and FC Groningen (the Netherlands), and Espanyol and Real Madrid (Spain). The problem is much bigger in Eastern Europe, however, where clubs like Dynamo Zagreb (Croatia), Ferencvaros (Hungary), Legia Warsaw (Poland), Spartak Moscow (Russia), and Karpaty Lviv (Ukraine) are notorious for their far-right support. Only a few non-European clubs are known for their far-right ultras. The best known is Beitar Jerusalem in Israel, whose far-right hooligans, known as *La Familia*, are infamous for their "Death to Arabs" chants.

Most West European states have clamped down on hooliganism in general, and far-right hooliganism in particular, through bans on far-right and hooligan symbols as well as stadium bans for violent fans in the late twentieth century. But in recent years, football hooligans have again become involved in far-right actions, mostly outside of football stadiums. For example, Chemnitz FC hooligans played a major role in anti-refugee demonstrations and violence in the East German city in 2018, while hooligans of Dutch club PSV were involved in attacks on anti-racist protesters at a *Sinterklaas* event in Eindhoven that same year. Football hooligans have also founded their own Islamphobic "anti-extremist" organizations, notably the British Democratic Football Lads Alliance and the German Hooligans Against Salafists, which have organized demonstrations with several thousands of participants.

Skinheads

The skinhead subculture emerged in London in the 1960s, as a working-class alternative to the middle-class hippie subculture. Building upon other subcultures, including the mostly black rude boys and the mostly white mods, the initial skinhead subculture was multiracial and relatively apolitical. Musically diverse, from ska to punk, skinheads stood out because of their shaved heads and a specific, and relatively strict, dress code, including Dr. Martens boots, Fred Perry polo shirts, bleached jeans, and narrow braces.

In the 1970s, part of the skinhead movement became increasingly associated with the far right, in particular Britain's National Front, which was one of the first anti-immigrant parties to contest elections in postwar Europe. NF activist Ian Stuart Donaldson (a.k.a. Ian Stuart) was instrumental in the creation of the far-right skinhead subculture, as was his band, Skrewdriver, whose record and song "White Power" is the unofficial anthem of the movement. Far-right skinheads developed a somewhat different dress code, shedding much of the rude boys' culture, but still look largely identical to other skinheads, including anti-racist skins (Skinheads Against Racial Prejudice), also known as "redskins."

Although most media conflate the skinhead movement with the far right, the vast majority of skinheads are non-political or anti-racist. The "Nazi skin" movement peaked in the 1980s in much of Western Europe, and in the 1990s in North America, and has declined sharply since. In part because of the negative public image of skinheads, far-right subcultures have increasingly diversified, and mainstreamed, in terms of music and style. Today, far-right skinheads mainly remain prominent in Eastern Europe, including in the Czech Republic, Poland, Russia, and Serbia. But there are even small neo-Nazi skin subcultures in non-white countries, including Mongolia and Malaysia.

In essence, the far-right skinhead movement is mainly a subculture, without strong organizations of its own, existing primarily online and mobilizing around specific concerts. It is built around a combination of cultural and political markers, expressions of which mainly exist online and around concerts in fashion and music.

International Collaboration

Despite alarmist accusations by some anti-fascists, and sensationalist stories by journalists, international collaborations between far-right activists and organizations have never been particularly successful. This applies to both the extreme right and the radical right, and for similar reasons. First, the far right has limited resources. Second, it is a very volatile political phenomenon, with only a few relatively stable organizations. Third, many groups have dominant leaders, who are not used to collaborating or sharing power. Fourth, while many far-right activists express serious interest in, and solidarity with, far-right brethren in other countries, their nationalism (and nativism) can lead to insurmountable differences of opinion. For instance, the Croatian and Serbian far right each dream of a largely similar territory – Greater Croatia for the former, Greater Serbia for the latter – while many West European far-right activists and groups look down on East Europeans, and several East European far-right groups are strongly anti-German.

International collaboration is intrinsic to neo-Nazis and white nationalists, whose "nation" is defined racially and therefore more internationally. But most of these groups already struggle to organize nationally, let alone internationally. Consequently, within the extreme right, international collaboration rarely goes beyond personal connections between a few specific individuals from Western Europe and North America, and sporadic events (like conferences and concerts), despite grandiose names like the World Union of National Socialists. In some cases, international collaboration is based more on a franchise model, where various "branches" use a similar name, but coordination and collaboration between the branches are minimal. This is particularly the case within the neo-Nazi skinhead world and applies to both the UK-centric Blood and Honour (B&H), founded by Ian Stuart Donaldson, and the US-centric Hammerskin Nation.

Only a few extreme right international collaborations have some relevance in the twenty-first century. The Nordic Resistance Movement (NMR) is a pan-Nordic neo-Nazi movement with branches in five Nordic countries: Denmark, Finland, Iceland, Norway, and Sweden – in the latter it is even a political party. While individual branches have at best modest support, they regularly mobilize dozens, and in Sweden hundreds, of mostly young people and have been linked to street violence. In 2017, the NMR mobilized some five hundred members in Sweden's second-largest city of Gothenburg, but in the same year its Finnish branch was banned by a district court.

The latest iteration of an extreme right Euro-party is the seriously misnamed Alliance for Peace and Freedom (APF), founded in 2015 and currently counting nine member parties from eight countries. Only two have national representations: L'SNS and XA are represented in both their respective national parliaments and the European Parliament. The APF's 2018 conference in Milan, Italy, was held in a fairly small room and featured speakers from eight marginal extreme right groups from Eastern and Western Europe.

The situation is only slightly better for the populist radical right. Most of the newer Islamophobic initiatives share (part of) a name rather than an organization. This applies to the various EDL-inspired "Defence Leagues," PEGIDAs, and Soldiers of Odin, a likely short-lived pan-European initiative of anti-Islam vigilantes. For decades, the FN/RN has been at the heart of collaboration between Europe's far-right parties, but with only modest success. Despite significant financial rewards for cross-national collaboration from the EU, populist radical right parties have always been divided and poorly organized within the European Parliament.

The Group of the European Right (1984–9) was the first official far-right group in the European Parliament, including just the MSI, FN, and the Greek National Political Union – for a short time the Ulster Unionist Party was also affiliated. It was succeeded by the Technical Group of the European Right (1989–94), in which the FN replaced the MSI with Germany's new The Republicans (REP), while the Belgian VB took the place of the Greeks, who did not get reelected. When REP lost its European representation in 1994, after years of infighting and splits, most remaining far-right MEPs sat as independents ("Non-Inscrits") for the subsequent terms – although some were accepted in broader right-wing Eurosceptic groups, like Independence/Democracy (LPR) and the Union for Europe of the Nations (e.g. DF and LN). To ensure an official political group, and its material benefits in the future, Jean-Marie Le Pen had founded Euronat in 1997, a loose and largely ineffective organization of which almost twenty far-right parties were a member at some point. Its first new attempt, the loose group Identity, Tradition, Sovereignty, was short-lived, from January till November 2007. Euronat was, for all purposes, succeeded by the European Alliance for Freedom (EAF) in 2010, which had at its core the FN, FPÖ, LN, PVV, and VB. But even though far-right parties won in the 2014 European elections, as they had done in 2009, it would take Marine Le Pen until 2015 to constitute a new official political group, Europe of Nations and Freedom (ENF). ENF replaced the EAF, which was officially dissolved in 2016, mainly by adding some dissident MEPs from assorted far-right parties. After the modestly successful 2019 European elections, the ENF is to be replaced by a new group, more aligned with Matteo Salvini than Marine Le Pen, which has attracted some new member parties (e.g. the AfD and the DF), but other parties prefer to stay in more established right-wing Eurosceptic groups – like the European People's Party (Fidesz), European Conservatives and Reformists (e.g. FvD, PiS), and Europe of Freedom and Direct Democracy (e.g. Brexit Party) – while extreme right MEPs remain in the Non-Inscrits group (L'SNS and XA).

Outside of Europe, international connections are mainly limited to fairly undeveloped and fluid networks of neo-Nazis. There are many personal connections between far-right activists, but they rarely develop into institutional collaboration. And even though both Russian president Putin and US president Trump are sympathetic to radical right parties and politics, they have largely kept their distance. Trump is only relatively close to ex-UKIP and now Brexit Party leader Nigel Farage, while Putin's (former) party United Russia has so far only signed official cooperation agreements with the FPÖ and the League. Israeli right-wing parties, including Likud, have recently strengthened ties to several European populist radical right parties (including Fidesz, LN, and PVV), but remain cautious towards the RN and continue to reject the FPÖ.

Vignette 2: CasaPound

Most far-right organizations fall within only one of these categories – political parties, social movement organizations, or subcultures – but some are more fluid, combining subcultural aspects with organizational structures and even contesting elections. A group that brings all three types of organization together is CasaPound Italy (CPI), which identifies itself as a "fascist movement." Named after the modernist poet and fascist ideologue Ezra Pound, CPI has its ideological origins in historical fascism, most notably the Labour Charter (1927) and the Manifesto of Verona (1943), although it emerged institutionally out of the neo-fascist subculture of postwar Italy.

Founded in 2003 as CasaPound, the group has its institutional origins in the squatting of a building in Rome. Taking its cue from the radical left squatting movement of previous decades, the group used its squat as a base to build a broader support base, housing activists and organizing

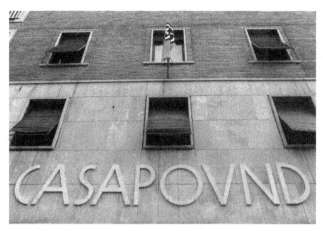

The squat-turned-headquarters of CasaPound Italy in Rome, Italy.
(Source: Jose Antonio/Italian Wikipedia/2014.)

concerts and lectures to the public. In 2008 it changed its name to CasaPound Italy and officially became a "social organization," to emphasize its focus on the housing issue and (nativist) welfare, that is, only for "real" Italians. Today CPI is present in almost all Italian regions, having more than 150 local branches, owning bookshops and pubs as well as online radio and TV channels. It publishes magazines like *Fare Quadrato* and *L'Occidentale*, as well as a new newspaper, *Il Primato Nazionale*, and has set up a network of "non-conventional" squats throughout Italy. It even has its own band, ZetaZeroAlfa (ZZA), founded by Gianluca Iannone, the founding father of CPI.

CPI counts several thousands of activists, including a youth wing, the Student Block. Since 2013, the group has also contested elections, national and local and regional, though so far with little success. In 2018, CPI gained just 1 percent of the vote in the parliamentary elections. In line with its fascist ideology and roots, the organization continues to prioritize extra-parliamentary activities, however, including social activities like providing food to (exclusively) Italian citizens. Given its emphasis on martial beliefs and behavior, it is unsurprising that CPI has been involved in political violence, including clashes with anti-fascists as well as terrorist attacks, like the killing of two Senegalese immigrants in Florence, in 2011, by a CPI sympathizer.

4

People

The far right consists not only of groups, but also of people. The international far right has two stereotypical types of supporters: the grumpy old, white racist – immortalized by the characters of Archie Bunker in the 1970s US sitcom *All in the Family* and Alf Garnett in the UK sitcom *Till Death Us Do Part* – and the heavily tattooed, violent, young Nazi skin, whose pictures accompany virtually every news story about the far right. What both have in common is that they are lower educated, white, male, and upset about "Others." While this particular section of the population is indeed overrepresented within the far right, the movement is, however, much more diverse. This chapter discusses the leaders, members and activists, and voters of the far right.

Leaders

Jean-Marie Le Pen (b. 1928) is in many ways the quintessential far-right leader: white (or majority ethnicity/

race), male, straight, older, authoritarian, charismatic, crude, violent, and with a military background. In his heyday, Le Pen was a mesmerizing speaker, drawing crowds in the thousands who paid to hear him speak. I saw him in Paris in 1986, during the only period the FN had a sizeable representation in parliament. The National Assembly was rather empty, as all other parties boycotted FN speeches, leaving just one MP to report back, so Le Pen was mainly grandstanding for his own faction. Thundering about the corruption of the "Gang of Four" (the other parties) and the dangers of multiculturalism, he captivated not just his own party representatives but many in the public stands too. Almost twenty years later, I saw him again, at an event organized by a student club in Ghent, Belgium. Le Pen was now old, bitter, and boring. He had overstayed his welcome by at least a decade.

Far-right leaders come in many types and only few are as powerful as Jean-Marie Le Pen used to be. To be fair, there is no shortage of the Le Pen-type of leader. Brazil's president Jair Bolsonaro (b. 1955) and XA leader Nikolaos Michaloliakos (b. 1957) are very similar to the French leader, both also having a military background, while US president Donald Trump (b. 1946) hits all the notes except for the military – Trump famously had five draft deferments to keep him out of the Vietnam War. But they are rapidly becoming a minority in an increasingly diverse pool of far-right leaders. Sure, the majority is still white, male, older, and straight, but so are most party leaders. In fact, far-right leaders are increasingly mirroring the leaders of mainstream parties in other aspects too: college-educated, professional politicians who have come through the ranks of the party.

Two good examples are Jimmie Åkesson and Tom Van Grieken, the leaders of Sweden's SD and Belgium's VB, respectively. Åkesson (b. 1979) was briefly active within the youth wing of the mainstream right Moderate Party

Donald Trump and Jair Bolsonaro hold a joint press conference in the Rose Garden of the White House in 2019. (Source: Official White House Photo by Tia Dufour/ Flickr/2019.)

before joining the SD youth wing. He was first elected at the age of nineteen to a local council, and has been a full-time party politician since. Similarly, Van Grieken (b. 1986) joined the VB at a young age, founded a youth branch in his home town, and got elected to his local council at the age of twenty. He then became leader of the national youth branch before moving up to national party leader a few years later. At just twenty-eight years old, he became the youngest party leader in Belgian history. Åkesson and Van Grieken are both products of their political party, and each helped mainstream their party with their idealized son-in-law image.

Most of the current leaders of successful populist radical right parties are a bit older but have fairly similar characteristics and trajectories. Matteo Salvini (b. 1973), who transformed Italy's moribund LN, comes from an upper-middle-class family, attended university

– although, like Åkesson, did not finish because he entered politics – and then worked full-time for the party. Norbert Hofer (b. 1971), who almost won the Austrian presidency for the FPÖ in 2016, grew up in an upper-middle-class, conservative household before working his way up through the ranks of the party, including as a close advisor to then party chairman Heinz-Christian Strache.

Outside of Europe, the profile is not that much different either. India's Narendra Modi (b. 1950) mainly differs from other leaders because of his modest family background, but he also joined the far-right movement at a (very) young age, and started working as a *pracharak* (campaigner) for the extremist RSS at the age of twenty-one. From there, he rose through the ranks of the RSS before being assigned to the BJP. Petrus (Pieter) Groenewald (b. 1955), leader of the white nationalist Freedom Front Plus in South Africa, joined the leading pro-apartheid National Party as a student, and built a long political career in a host of pro-apartheid parties before co-founding his own party in 1994. Similarly, Antonio Kast (b. 1966) was a long-time member and parliamentarian for the conservative Independent Democratic Union in Chile, before running as an independent in the 2017 presidential election (winning 10 percent of the vote) and founding the radical right movement Republican Action in 2018. And Naftali Bennett (b. 1972) was first active within Likud, including as Benjamin Netanyahu's chief of staff, before founding several far-right movements and ultimately joining and leading Jewish Home and then New Right.

But not all far-right leaders fit the stereotype. First and foremost, there is a growing group of female party leaders (see also chapter 9). Most famous among them, of course, is Marine Le Pen (b. 1968), Jean-Marie's youngest daughter, and his hand-picked successor within the RN – a choice he has openly regretted many times since, as she has marginalized both him and his legacy. Against the inherited leadership of Le Pen stand the self-made careers of women like Pia Kjærsgaard (b. 1947) and Pauline Hanson (b. 1954), founders and longtime leaders of Denmark's DF and Australia's ONP, respectively. Even some extreme right organizations have (had) female (deputy) leaders, like Jayda Fransen (b. 1986) of Britain First and Anne Marie Waters (b. 1977) of For Britain.

There are even some leaders who are (more or less) openly gay, albeit it more in right-wing populist parties than in more traditional far-right parties. The most famous openly gay leaders were undoubtedly Pim Fortuyn (b. 1948), who was murdered weeks before his first Dutch national election in 2002, and Michael Kühnen (b. 1955), the notorious leader of Germany's Action Front of National Socialists/National Activists (ANS/NA), who died of AIDS in 1991. Currently, the most high-profile gay far-right leader is Alice Weidel (b. 1979), who leads the Alternative for Germany (AfD) together with Alexander Gauland. Weidel is probably the most atypical far-right leader today: female and lesbian, she worked for Goldman Sachs and speaks Mandarin, and lives partly abroad (in Switzerland) with her non-white partner, who was born in Sri Lanka, and their two adopted children.

Finally, there are even leaders who are not part of the majority ethnic or racial group. This is virtually impossible in the more openly racist extreme right groups, but less problematic within primarily Islamophobic radical right groups. Here, the almost exclusively "Other" is the Muslim, and the "us" is defined in terms of both national and international characteristics, that is, "Judeo-Christian values." Hence, one of the key EDL organizers was a British Sikh, Guramit Singh Kalirai, while an "Afro-Cuban" man, Enrique Tarrio, is president of the Miami chapter of the extreme right "Western chauvinist" Proud Boys group.

Some even make it to national leader, such as Tomio Okamura (b. 1972), who was born in Tokyo to a half-Japanese, half-Korean father and a Czech mother. After growing up in Japan, he moved to the Czech Republic, where he started various more or less successful businesses before embarking on a political career. Okamura was elected as an independent to the Czech Senate in 2012 and created his own party, Tomio Okamura's Dawn of Direct Democracy, a year later. After successful national elections in 2013, the party split, and Okamura founded a new party, Freedom and Democracy, which became the most successful populist radical right party in Czech history in 2017. Okamura has used his own ethnic background as a cover against racism accusations over his bigoted statements, such as calling upon Czechs to walk their pigs in front of mosques.

Members and Activists

Political organizations are notoriously secretive about their membership, in terms of both identity and numbers. This is even more the case for far-right organizations, which assume, rightly, that their members want to remain anonymous because of the associated stigma. Consequently, we have little systematic research on the topic. Most studies are based on interviews with an unrepresentative sample of more dedicated members, namely activists, or participant observations of far-right meetings.

Over the years, I have observed several far-right meetings myself, ranging from demonstrations and party meetings to more casual social meetings, like barbeques and concerts. My personal impressions largely overlap with those of others, albeit with some national and organizational particularities. Overall, activists in Europe seem to be almost exclusively white, predominantly male, and lower middle class rather than working class. In terms of age, there was a big difference between extreme right groups (mostly youngish) and radical right parties (mostly older, i.e. fifty-five-plus). An early study of the small and short-lived populist radical right Center Democrats in the Netherlands, for example, found that its members were predominantly male, older, working class, non-religious, and from the more urbanized west of the country.[1] A survey among participants of LN and SVP rallies found fairly similar profiles, although they were not as old, and LN participants were better educated than at least the average far-right voter.[2]

Membership in non-party organizations is even harder to track. Not only are these groups much smaller, less organized, and often local or at best regional, but their "members" tend to be transient, with people moving in and out of specific groups and sometimes even the broader subculture. Most studies find that groups that are more extreme in terms of actions and ideology, most notably violent neo-Nazi groups, are even more predominantly male and working class, and tend to be much younger, that is, on average between fifteen and twenty-five years old, with the exception of the leadership, who are often in their thirties and early forties. While women are present, they often have more supportive roles, both to the male members and, if relevant, to their children (see chapter 9).

The picture is a bit different for online-oriented organizations, although anonymity makes this group even harder to study. A Japanese study of a small number of *Netto Uyoku* (Internet right-wing) activists found that the vast majority were white collar, had a regular form of employment, and were enrolled in university or had been at one time. An online study of US "alt-right" supporters showed that they were predominantly male (two-thirds) and white (almost all), while three-quarters had voted for Donald Trump in 2016.[3]

Scholars have distinguished different trajectories of far-right activists, depending on why they joined and remained active. They distinguish, for example, between *revolutionaries*, who have a lifelong commitment to far-right politics; *converts*, who used to believe, and sometimes were active, in mainstream politics before converting to far-right politics; *wanderers*, who have been active within a broad variety of far-right and non-far-right groups; and *compliants*, who claim that their far-right activism is not of their own choosing but because of circumstances beyond their control – most often family connections. The largest group among members (and voters) is the converts, whereas leaders are more often revolutionaries. Compliants are more common among women than men (see also chapter 9).

Voters

Since the beginning of the third wave in the early 1980s, scholars have been studying the electoral support of far-right parties in detail. This section discusses the attitudinal and socio-demographic characteristics of far-right supporters – their motivations will be addressed in more detail in chapter 6. The "typical" voter of far-right parties in Western Europe is white, male, young(ish), moderately educated, and concerned about immigrants and immigration. However, the typical far-right voter constitutes only a minority of the electorate of far-right parties, particularly for the more successful parties. Moreover, in most countries, a majority of people with these characteristics vote for parties other than those of the far right.

West European far-right parties initially attracted small groups of dissatisfied, mainstream right-wing voters, disproportionately petty bourgeois and self-employed men. Their electoral breakthrough in the 1990s was a consequence of the "proletarianization" of their electorates. Parties like the FN and FPÖ became workers' parties, as growing numbers of white workers increasingly felt abandoned, if not outright betrayed, by social democratic parties, whose "Third Way" transformation included not just an embrace of the market economy but also a defense of cosmopolitan values. In fact, in the late 1990s, both parties were more popular among (white) workers than the social democratic parties in their respective countries. Today, even smaller parties, like the AfD and PVV, are among the stronger "workers' parties" in their respective countries.

As far-right parties are becoming more and more successful, their electorates keep transforming, becoming increasingly heterogenous. Already in the early 1990s, French scholars would divide the FN electorate into different groups, based on their previous voting behavior and political attitudes, including the more working-class "leftist Lepenists," the largely amorphous "neither/nor-ists (*ninistes*)," and the predominantly (petty-)bourgeois "rightists."[4] Others differentiate between "protest" and "support" voters, based on whether they mainly vote *for* the far right or *against* the other parties (see also chapter 6). The situation is even more complex in conservative-turned-radical right parties, like Fidesz or the SVP, let alone for mainstream parties run by far-right leaders, like Bolsonaro and Trump, which combine characteristics of both electorates. For instance, one recent study[5] distinguished between five types of Trump voters: American Preservationists (20 percent), Staunch Conservatives (31 percent), Free Marketeers (25 percent), Anti-Elites (19 percent), and the Disengaged (5 percent). While the last two fit with general far-right electorates, the first three more resemble conservative electorates.

In short, the more popular the far-right group, the more diverse its support base. While the public image of *the* far-right supporter is still a stereotypical white, working-class man, the far right draws leaders, activists, and voters from all walks of life. And the most successful populist radical right parties have transformed from working-class parties in the third wave to so-called "*Volksparteien*" (people's parties), reflecting almost all subgroups of the population, in the fourth wave.

5

Activities

The far right engages in three main types of activities: elections, demonstrations, and violence. Populist radical right parties usually attract rather modest crowds in demonstrations, but increasingly large numbers of voters in elections. In contrast, extreme right groups rarely contest elections successfully, if at all, and attract usually even smaller numbers onto the streets. And where populist radical right parties and groups tend to be primarily non-violent, extreme right activists and groups are more often involved in political violence.

For much of the postwar period, organized far-right terrorist groups were rare, as far-right political violence remained mostly limited to more or less random and spontaneous attacks by far-right mobs – with the exception of more organized anti-immigrant and anti-Roma "pogroms" in East Germany and Eastern Europe in the 1990s. In the wake of the so-called "refugee crisis" (2015) in Europe, and the election of Donald Trump (2016) in the US, far-right demonstrations and rallies have increased in frequency and size, while political violence has become more common and deadly. After decades of being blind in the right eye, worsened by the obsessive focus on jihadi terrorism after 9/11, law enforcement and intelligence agencies in a growing number of countries are now warning against the growing threat of far-right terrorism.

Elections

Elections are the most important form of mobilization within democracies. They determine who will represent us and, therefore, are the ultimate forum for achieving political influence. But they are also a great way to achieve visibility in the media, given that elections always receive close coverage. Finally, elections provide an opportunity to attain significant financial resources.

While election campaigns cost political parties money, in many countries they are compensated by the state, often based on either the number of votes or the number of seats they receive in (national) elections. Moreover, once parties gain representation in legislative bodies, at the national, subnational, or supranational level, they have access to even more media coverage and financial resources. Particularly for many far-right activists, being a legislator, or even legislative assistant, is a fairly easy and well-paid job compared to their non-political careers.

Almost all far-right parties contest elections, although some smaller, often extreme right parties do so only intermittently. For example, the Icelandic National Front contested the 2016 national election, but withdrew from the 2017 national elections. On average, far-right parties currently gain around 7.5 percent of the national vote in Europe (see the table below). Their results range from just a handful of votes to an outright majority of the electorate. For instance, Identity Ireland got less than 0.05 percent in the 2016 Irish elections (a grand

Average vote (%) for far-right parties in National and European parliamentary elections in EU member states, 1980–2018 (by decade)

Decade	National elections	European elections
1980–9	1.1	2.4
1990–9	4.4	4.3
2000–9	4.7	5.6
2010–18	7.5	7.6

Source: Parlgov.

total of 181 votes overall), yet Fidesz won 49.3 percent in the 2018 Hungarian elections.

It is broadly believed that far-right parties do better in second-order elections than in first-order elections: that is, elections that determine the constitution of the national executive. The idea is that people vote with their heart when it matters, but with their boot when it does not. However, on average, far-right parties achieve relatively similar scores in elections for the national (first-order) and European (second-order) parliament. They tend to do worse in local and regional elections, mainly because many far-right parties do not have the institutional capacity to contest elections across the country. At the same time, they often peak in traditional local strongholds in subnational elections, such as in Antwerp in Belgium (VB), Gujarat in India (BJP), Nord-Pas-de-Calais-Picardie in France (RN), or Skåne in Sweden (SD).

The most successful far-right parties today are often former mainstream right-wing parties that have transformed into populist radical right ones. East Central European parties like Fidesz and PiS are among the most recent examples, but they were preceded by the FPÖ and SVP in Western Europe. Outside of the

European context, Likud in Israel is an important, but often overlooked, case. These parties profit from a so-called "reputational shield," that is, their origins protect them from a far-right stigma, as at least part of the national, and international, media and politics continue to perceive them as conservative long after their transformation into the populist radical right. In most cases, their radicalization has helped rather than hurt them in elections.

Far-right candidates often do better in presidential elections than their party does in parliamentary elections, but they rarely win. The most successful far-right politicians ran as candidates for a non-radical right party, like Jair Bolsonaro of the Social Liberal Party in Brazil and Donald Trump of the Republican Party in the US. Because they polarize the population, meaning that most people either really like or dislike them, far-right politicians tend to be unsuccessful in systems that use a two-round majoritarian system. The best example is France, where both Jean-Marie (2002) and Marine Le Pen (2017) made it into the second round but were then soundly defeated. However, even here things are changing, as FPÖ candidate Norbert Hofer was only narrowly defeated in the second round of the 2016 Austrian presidential elections.

Far-right groups and parties have mixed successes in referendums. Many countries set high thresholds for referendums, which means the far right is unable to organize a referendum, or people's initiative, by itself. In 1993, the FPÖ tried to organize an anti-immigration "Austria First" referendum, which remained not more than a modestly successful petition. In 2016, several populist radical right activists and groups in the Netherlands successfully forced the reluctant Dutch government to organize an advisory referendum on the Ukraine–EU Association Agreement. Although they won the valid referendum, with 61 percent voting against the Agreement and a 32 percent turnout, the Dutch government by and large ignored the outcome. However, the campaign became the launch pad of several successful and unsuccessful political careers, most notably that of Thierry Baudet and his FvD.

The most organic relationship between the far right and referendums exists in Switzerland, famous for its direct democracy. Although the SVP is officially part of the Swiss government, a peculiarity of the Swiss Constitution, it regularly uses popular initiatives (*Volksinitiative*) to try to block national and local legislation, particularly with regard to EU membership and immigration. SVP strongman Christoph Blocher even co-founded a special organization for this purpose in 1986, the Campaign for an Independent and Neutral Switzerland, which, although officially non-partisan, has long acted hand in glove with the SVP in its campaigns.

Demonstrations

For many far-right organizations, particularly those not contesting elections, demonstrations are their most important activity. The German scholar Fabian Virchow has described demonstrations and marches as "politico-emotional events" which perform a multitude of important functions for the groups participating. They "not only bring together otherwise loosely organized small groups in an emotional collective but also serve to organize, educate, and indoctrinate the followers of the far right."[1]

Different demonstrations perform different functions and require different levels of mobilization and organization. Larger groups and movements (hope to) organize large demonstrations to influence public opinion through the media and put political pressure

XA protest in Athens, Greece, 2017.
(Photo by author.)

on mainstream parties. Smaller groups often organize relatively small events, involving only a few activists, with the exclusive aim of attracting the attention of the mainstream media, which will then spread their message to a much broader audience. The Identitarian movement is particularly adept at staging mediagenic events (see vignette 3). More extreme groups, like the NMR in Scandinavia or the Proud Boys in the US, organize demonstrations largely to provoke confrontations with anti-fascists and the police, in an attempt to strengthen an almost military camaraderie through action (see also chapter 9).

A typical extreme right demonstration in Western Europe is held in a provincial town, gathering a few dozen activists, almost all (white) males between fifteen and forty years old, surrounded by at least as many (riot) police, even more (freelance) journalists, and at least twice as many "anti-fascist" counter-protesters. Radical right demonstrations can attract larger crowds, and fewer counter-protesters, but still tend to be remarkably rare and small, particularly given the media hype surrounding them. While far-right groups have organized demonstrations on many different issues, such as against austerity measures in Italy or against the Obama administration in the US, they are mostly related to immigration and integration.

Anti-Islam demonstrations have become a common occurrence throughout Europe, but not only there (see, e.g., India or Israel). There are two groups that have become synonymous with these demonstrations, the EDL in the UK and PEGIDA in Germany, which have inspired dozens of offshoots in their own countries and beyond, such as the Canadian Defence League and Norwegian Defence League, or LEGIDA (in Leipzig, Germany) and PEGIDA USA. In reality, few if any of these offshoots have come close to the success of the original. This itself, however, was already quite limited: the EDL never brought more than 3,000 people onto the streets for a single demonstration, while PEGIDA peaked at some 25,000 in Dresden.

In Eastern Europe, far-right demonstrations can be significantly bigger and largely unopposed. This is in part because they act under the cloak of respectability, attracting both far-right and mainstream protesters. For example, in 2017, some 60,000 people attended the annual Independence Day march in Warsaw, which was led by three far-right groups. The next year, for the centenary of Polish independence, the PiS government joined the far-right-organized march, rather than organizing its own, and the crowd peaked at around 200,000. And in Ukraine, tens of thousands of far-right activists regularly march through the streets of Kyiv, sometimes in torchlight processions, to commemorate old and new far-right heroes, including those of the neo-Nazi Azov Battalion, which fights against the Russian-backed occupation of Crimea.

In the wake of the "refugee crisis," we have seen a sharp increase in bottom-up and spontaneous anti-refugee protests. Many of these demonstrations were purely local in scope, with one single issue: preventing the settlement of (new) refugees in the community. While far-right groups often tried to hijack these protests, after they were reported in national or regional media, many local protesters would reject them as "extremists" and/or "outsiders." Particularly in East Central Europe, small, local, spontaneous protests grew into larger, national demonstrations. New or old far-right groups often played an important role in the mobilization and organization of these rallies. For example, the organizer of the main anti-refugee demonstration in Bratislava in 2015, one of the biggest postcommunist demonstrations ever held in the Slovak capital, worked closely together with the neo-fascist ĽSNS, while, at a rally in Prague the same year, the leader of the (now dissolved) Bloc Against Islam sang the national anthem together with Czech president Miloš Zeman, a former social democrat who has more recently moved to the radical right.

Outside of Europe, far-right demonstrations have become more popular too. After deteriorating relations between Japan and South Korea, the anti-Korean activist online group Zaitokukai organized more than a thousand rallies throughout Japan between April 2012 and September 2015. Although most rallies were relatively small in terms of attendance, some turned violent, and the movement enjoyed (tacit) support among high-ranking politicians of the dominant Liberal Democratic Party. In India, the large Hindutva movement regularly pulls off massive demonstrations. For example, in 2018, in Kolkata, some 70,000 people assembled to mark the tenth anniversary of the founding of the anti-Muslim Hindu Samhati nationalist movement. In Brazil, the run-up to the 2018 presidential elections saw huge rallies in support of Bolsonaro across the country. In contrast, while Trump has attracted decent crowds at his rallies, both before and after his election, pro-Trump demonstrations rarely achieve impressive numbers, particularly compared to the anti-Trump demonstrations.

Violence

The far right is commonly associated with violence, be it larger populist radical right parties or smaller extreme right groups and individuals. However, those who primarily perpetrate far-right violence have traditionally not been the leaders within politically relevant organizations but (small groups of) individuals who have at best a peripheral association with the far-right movement. Nevertheless, in recent years far-right violence has become more planned, regular, and lethal, as terrorist attacks in, among others, Christchurch (New Zealand), Pittsburgh (US), and Utøya (Norway) show. And in the wake of the "refugee crisis," more and more countries are growing increasingly concerned about the rise of far-right terrorist groups such as the German National Socialist Underground.

There are a few far-right parties for which political violence is an integral part of their action repertoire. The Greek neo-Nazi party XA has been linked to a string of violent attacks on immigrants and political opponents. The party is even accused of having (had) a secret shadow organization to attack people perceived as "enemies of the Greek nation." The youth wing of the Turkish MHP, commonly known as the Grey Wolves, has terrorized party opponents in Turkey as well as Turkish emigrant communities abroad. And Rabbi Kahane's Kach party in Israel started as a violent group in the US, the Jewish Defense League, which was involved in several terrorist attacks. Today, it remains active in several countries, and members have been linked to political violence in Canada and France, among other countries.

In many countries (including Germany, India, Sweden, and the US), the far right has been responsible for more political violence than the far left, or than ethnic and religious minorities. The Norwegian terrorism scholar Jacob Aasland Ravndal[2] of the Center for Research on Extremism (C-REX) at the University of Oslo calculated that there were 578 far-right violent incidents in Western Europe in the period 1990–2015, including 190 deadly incidents causing 303 deaths. During roughly the same period in the US (1990–2013), far-right activists killed 368 individuals in a total of 155 ideologically motivated homicides.[3] Of course, this only scratches the surface of the real violence, or the threat thereof, let alone its perception by targeted communities.

Most far-right violence (i.e. violence inspired by far-right ideas) targets people who are perceived as "aliens" (e.g. ethnic minorities, immigrants, refugees) or "degenerates" (e.g. [alleged] feminists, gays, leftists, homeless people). The stereotypical perpetrator is a young(ish) white male, often intoxicated, who attacks the victim in a quasi-spontaneous manner. Sometimes larger groups of individuals go on quasi-spontaneous violent rampages, triggered by local incidents or rumors. Anti-Roma pogroms have a long history in East Central Europe, as do anti-Muslim and anti-Sikh pogroms in India. And as noted in chapter 3, in 2018, a violent mob led by football hooligans went on a hunt for "foreigners" in the East German city of Chemnitz after a Cuban-German man was stabbed to death following an altercation with two suspected refugees.

Far-right terrorism has become a growing threat in recent years. So-called "lone wolves," presumed solitary actors, who are nevertheless often significantly influenced by broader far-right subcultures, particularly online, have committed the bulk of the high-profile cases of far-right terrorism. The Norwegian terrorist who killed seventy-seven and injured 319 in an Oslo bombing and Utøya shooting spree in 2010 published a long, ranting "manifesto" that drew heavily from populist radical right politicians and far-right online sources.[4] And the Australian terrorist who killed fifty and seriously wounded fifty more at two mosques in Christchurch (New Zealand) in 2019 actually named his manifesto "The Great Replacement," after a conspiracy theory popular with both conservative and far-right circles (see chapter 3). Some "lone wolves" were actually linked to actual far-right organizations, like the failed LN candidate who injured six immigrants during a shooting spree in Macerata (Italy) in 2018.

The most infamous recent example of a true far-right terrorist organization was the National Socialist Underground in Germany, which consisted of three core members, and is held responsible for ten murders, three bombings, and fourteen bank robberies. In the UK, the neo-Nazi group National Action was officially banned as a terrorist organization in 2016 after many of its members had been accused, and some convicted, of threatening or using violence against minorities and political opponents. In France, in 2018, the authorities dismantled a small far-right terrorist group, the Operational Forces Action, which was believed to be on the verge of carrying out terrorist attacks against Muslims in the country. And in India, the Hindu extremist group Abhinav Bharat, deemed too extremist even by the Sangh Parivar, has been linked to several deadly bombings between 2006 and 2008.

Far-right paramilitary groups are particularly prone to political violence, including outright terrorism. Most European paramilitary units are uniformed but (officially) not armed. Several were set up by far-right political parties, such as the Hungarian Guard, the banned but still operating paramilitary wing of Jobbik; the LN's Green Shirts (*camicie verdi*) in Northern Italy; and the National Party's National Guard in the Czech Republic. While these groups rarely engage in overt physical violence, their mere presence – in formation, often wearing black uniforms with black boots, carrying torches and accompanied by dogs – is aimed at terrorizing targeted populations (mostly immigrants and Roma).

Similarly, in the wake of the "refugee crisis" several new militias emerged in Europe. For example, the Soldiers of Odin have been "patrolling" the streets in cities in several West European countries, mostly in Scandinavia, while in Central and Eastern Europe, groups like the Czech National Home Guard and the Slovenian Stajerska Gang claim to protect local populations against immigrants and refugees. The situation is most dangerous in Ukraine, however, where activists who fight within openly far-right units like the Azov Battalion, now integrated into the Ukrainian National Guard, have started to threaten to use their war experience and weapons "to use force to establish order that will bring prosperity to every Ukrainian family!"

US paramilitary units, more broadly known as militias, are always heavily armed because of the country's gun culture and lax firearms laws. Right-wing militias soared in the 1990s, but decreased significantly in the wake of the Oklahoma City Bombing of 1995. Under President Barack Obama, the number of militias again rose sharply, while they have been further emboldened by Trump's presidency. Traditionally, militias have been strongly anti-government, particularly towards the federal government, and many have been involved in threats and violence against the (federal) state and its representatives. However, when Trump entered the White House, many militias changed from anti-government to pro-government, at least staunchly pro-president. Some (new) groups, like the Oath Keepers and Three Percenters, have even threatened violence if President Trump were to be impeached. There is significant overlap with the so-called "sovereign citizens" movement, a very loose network of individuals and groups who believe that the local sheriff is the highest authority in the land. Sovereign citizens have been responsible for dozens of shootings in the US, mostly in response to arrest attempts or traffic stops by law enforcement agents. Germany has an equivalent in the form of the *Reichsbürgerbewegung* (Reich Citizens' Movement), who reject the legitimacy of the Federal Republic of Germany and believe the Weimar Constitution of 1919 is still valid. While much less armed and deadly than its US brethren, *Reichsbürger* have been involved in several shoot-outs with law enforcement too.

Arguably, the most powerful violent far-right group in the world is the RSS, a paramilitary organization with a claimed membership of 5–6 million, which is very close to India's ruling BJP. The RSS was banned under British rule and was outlawed three times following independence because of its involvement in political violence and terrorism. The last RSS ban was in 1992, lifted a year later, because of its alleged role in the demolition of the Babri Masjid mosque, which led to various ensuing riots with a total death toll of some 2,000. Since the BJP regained power in 2014, Hindutva militants, often organized within the myriad of RSS groups, have been prominently involved in violence against perceived national enemies, including eaters of cow meat – the cow is a holy animal in the Hindu faith – and the largest religious minority in the country, Muslims.

Vignette 3: The Identitarians

The Identitarians are a pan-European far-right movement which started with the Identitarian Bloc in France in 2003. The movement only took off internationally with the founding of its youth wing, Generation Identity, in 2012. It is currently active across Europe, including in Austria, the Czech Republic, Germany, Ireland, Italy, and the UK. Although various US "alt-right" groups don the Identitarian mantle, like Identity Evropa, there are significant ideological differences, and personal connections are relatively limited and strained – with some exceptions, such as US activist Brittany Pettibone and Canadian activist Lauren Southern.

Ideologically, the Identitarian movement is derived from the *nouvelle droite*, inspired by its main thinkers, Alain De Benoist and the late

Austrian Identitarian movement activists block the border crossing near Spielfeld, Austria, in 2015. (Source: Johanna Poetsch/istock/2015.)

Guillaume Faye. They present themselves as an anti-'68 movement, opposing the "cultural Marxism" and "multiculturalism" of the "left-liberal elite." As a product of the twenty-first century, however, their main "Other" is the Muslim, who is officially opposed on cultural grounds. The central agenda of the Identitarian movement is to oppose the alleged "Islamization" of Europe and to renew the birth rate and identity of European nations. Or, in the words of Markus Willinger, one of its key activists, "We don't want Mehmed and Mustafa to become Europeans." While it officially subscribes to ethnopluralism, and its slogan is "0 percent racism, 100 percent identity," the boundaries between biological and cultural arguments in the movement have become increasingly porous.

Although the *nouvelle droite* has always remained a purely "intellectual" movement, to the frustration of many less intellectual, and particularly younger, supporters, the Identitarian movement is much more diverse in its forms of mobilization. On the one hand, a few Identitarian groups and (former) leaders have contested elections, including in Croatia and France, if so far without any success. On the other hand, while rejecting accusations of extremism and violence, the movement's supporters have been accused of threatening left-wing activists and critical journalists, and the German Federal Office for the Protection of the Constitution is officially surveilling the group because it believes its activities "go against the liberal basic democratic order."

The Identitarian trademark action is a short, mediagenic protest, in which small groups of activists (often just a handful) generate significant media attention by briefly occupying a popular public space – often by exposing a large banner with a short and catchy slogan, symbols unrelated to the classic far right, and easily recognizable colors and fonts. Many journalists are completely enamored with the Identitarians, labeling them "hipster fascists" and providing them with disproportionate and fairly uncritical coverage. The movement's biggest action to date was "Defend Europe," where they crowdsourced more than $178,000 to purchase a large ship (renamed *C-Star*) in an attempt to obstruct human rights organizations from helping refugees in the Mediterranean Sea. Although the action was an organizational disaster, it achieved its prime goal: generating massive media attention.

6

Causes

The academic and public discussions over the reasons behind the success of the far right entail various debates, which resurface across different geographical regions and time periods with depressing frequency. The election of Donald Trump saw many of these old debates being rehashed, in particular in the US, often with no knowledge of or reference to the volumes of articles and books already devoted to them in Europe in the 1990s or even in the US in the 1960s.

In most cases, positions in the debates are not as fundamentally opposed as their protagonists make them out to be. Some are actually interrelated, at times to the extent that they can barely be disentangled empirically, while others are complementary, explaining different subsets of far-right support. In the first section, I discuss four of the most prominent debates: protest versus support; economic anxiety versus cultural backlash; global versus local; and leader versus organization. The second section focuses on the demand side of far-right politics, arguing that, while the extreme right is fairly unconnected to mainstream politics, the populist radical right is better seen as a radicalization of mainstream politics. The chapter ends with a discussion of the role of the media, which functions as both a friend and foe of the far right.

The Debates

It is no surprise that a controversial and polarizing phenomenon like the far right would give way to longstanding and heated debates in both academia and the broader public. While most of these debates are universal in nature, they are shockingly national in terms of detail. As a consequence, people are reinventing the wheel after every breakthrough of a far-right party in a new country, drawing few, if any, lessons from debates and experiences in other countries. This was most painfully shown in the wake of the rise of Donald Trump, which brought these debates to the center of political debates around the globe.

Protest versus Support

The first time I came across this debate was more than thirty-five years ago, after the tiny radical right Center Party had gained almost 10 percent of the vote in the Dutch city of Almere, at that time unflatteringly known as a "white flight" town for the Amsterdam working and middle classes. As the Netherlands had long defined itself as a uniquely non-nationalist country, covering its own history of collaboration in the Second World War with an obsessive focus on Nazi Germany, the success of the Center Party took the country by surprise and caused a major shock and discussion among politicians and pundits alike.

The key question of the protest versus support debate is: do voters of far-right parties express mainly protest *against* the established parties or support *for* the far-right parties? The idea is that a protest voter does not really believe in a far-right ideology, but uses the far-right party to protest against the behavior and policies of the established parties. In contrast, the support voter actually holds far-right ideas and has chosen the far-right party because it is closest to his/her own ideology.

Academic studies show that many voters of far-right parties are very dissatisfied with (established) political parties, but even more are very negative about immigration and immigrants. Obviously, many voters of other parties hold xenophobic sentiments too – particularly, but not exclusively, voters of mainstream right-wing parties – while anti-establishment senti- ments are even more widespread among non-voters. But far-right parties tend to have higher percentages of anti-establishment and anti-immigration voters than all other parties. Some studies also show that these senti- ments are more important to them than to voters of other parties.

In short, most studies provide circumstantial evidence for both the protest and the support thesis. This is not at all surprising. There is a perfectly logical third position, namely that voters of far-right parties *both* protest against the established parties *and* support the far-right parties. After all, when someone holds far-right ideas, they will not just support the party that holds those ideas, but also oppose the parties that hold opposite ideas. Moreover, protest voters can become support voters when they see the far-right party achieving policies they support.

It is important to note that the protest versus support debate is not politically neutral. Many people argue that protest is a morally acceptable position, whereas

A banner in California as remnant of Donald Trump's successful presidential campaign of 2016. (Source: Quinn Dombrowski/Flickr/2016.)

support is not. From the Center Party in the Netherlands in 1983 to Donald Trump in the US in 2016, debates about "far-right voters" have been battlegrounds for mainstream politicians and pundits to push through their own political agenda. Many on the protest side reduce *the* far-right voter to a white, working-class male who has "legitimate concerns" over his cultural identity and economic position. In contrast, many on the support side of the debate paint a similarly stereotypical far-right voter as an ideological racist who scapegoats "the Other" for his/her own (perceived) woes. This leads us to the second key debate.

Economic Anxiety versus Cultural Backlash

Simply stated, this debate is about whether people vote for far-right parties because of economic or cultural reasons. The economic anxiety argument holds that far-right voters are first and foremost responding to economic stress caused by "neoliberal globalization." Whether they are objectively poor or simply feel poor, these stereotypical far-right voters are seen as the "losers of globalization" who protest against their absolute or relative deprivation. The cultural backlash argument holds that these far-right voters mainly protest against another aspect of neoliberal globalization, namely mass immigration and the rise of a multicultural society, which they believe threatens their cultural identity.

It is clear that both theories have much in common, most notably the root cause of the phenomenon (i.e. neoliberal globalization), and see the far-right vote mainly as a protest, although cultural backlash proponents in particular don't exclude the possibility of support either. Decades of academic research have shown that cultural backlash is much more important than economic anxiety, and more recent research on the Trump electorate has once again confirmed this. In short, there are few far-right voters who are informed only by economic anxiety, while there are many who are only expressing a cultural backlash.

But the two are much more complementary than opposite. It is the socio-cultural translation of socio-economic concerns that explains most support for far-right politics. Egged on by nativist narratives in the political and public debates (e.g. "immigrants are taking your jobs *and* your benefits"), many far-right voters link immigration to economic problems, either for them personally or for the region or state they live in. Consequently, they think that limiting immigration, or assimilating immigrants, will improve their economic plight. This is most clearly expressed in welfare chauvinism, that is, the support for a welfare state for one's "own people," which is a major issue for most far-right parties and voters alike.

Global versus Local

The third debate is, again, connected to the previous ones, but focuses primarily on the locus of explanation: that is, whether the phenomenon is primarily global or local. In the most extreme terms, some people explain support for the far right in exclusively, or primarily, general terms, while others believe that each far-right group has to be explained individually and uniquely. Broadly stated, global arguments prioritize the demand side of far-right politics, such as economic anxiety and cultural backlash, while local arguments emphasize supply-side factors, like a charismatic leader and party organization (see below).

The most popular global argument is (neoliberal) globalization. As the most recent iteration of modernization theory, it entails that globalization has caused winners and losers and the latter vote for far-right parties either to punish the established parties (protest), which they hold responsible for globalization, or to put a halt to globalization (including immigration) and "get our country back" (support). Unsurprisingly, global arguments are mostly used by those who try to explain *the* success of the far right – recently more popularly referred to as "the rise of populism" – ignoring other globalized countries that do not have successful far-right parties (e.g. Ireland or Japan).

Local arguments primarily focus on the so-called "Political Opportunity Structure" (POS) within which far-right organizations operate, such as the electoral system and the legal framework. They also emphasize the supply side of far-right politics, including the behavior of both mainstream and far-right groups. For example, scholars have long agreed that openly extreme right parties could not succeed in the postwar era, but recent electoral successes by neo-Nazi parties like XA and L'SNS have proven this to be untrue. Similarly, the idea that majoritarian "first-past-the-post" electoral systems provide an effective barrier to far-right politics has been weakened by the recent elections of Bolsonaro and Trump.

There is no doubt that global factors help to explain why far-right politics can find more or less receptive audiences during certain time periods and in particular geographical regions, but far-right success is first and foremost a consequence of political supply, most notably from far-right leaders and organizations themselves. Even when unemployment and immigration levels are high, they must be defined as a threat to the national identity or state, and caused by "Others," to profit far-right actors. Quite often it is not far-right actors who do this, but rather tabloid media and opportunistic mainstream politicians, without necessarily arguing that far-right organizations provide solutions. In fact, they often combine support for a radical right narrative with opposition to radical right organizations – see, for example, *Bild Zeitung* in Germany or *The Sun* in the UK.

But the mainstream media and mainstream politics have created a fertile breeding ground for far-right groups to exploit by putting their issues at the top of the agenda and framing them in their way (see chapter 7). So we are not just talking about immigration, rather than about education or health care, but we are talking about it as a "problem" or even a "threat." This legitimizes far-right groups, but also makes them look competent, as they have been saying this for years and most of their programs deal with this exact issue. When mainstream parties fail to deliver on issues like crime and immigration, either by choice or through incompetence, far-right parties become attractive alternatives. If far-right parties can offer relatively serious leaders, organizations, and propaganda, rather than small bands of infighting hooligans, they can become an attractive alternative for those voters most concerned about these issues.

Leader versus Organization

The fourth debate shifts the focus to the internal supply side of far-right politics, that is, what the far right offers potential supporters. Discussions about the far right traditionally put much emphasis on "the leader," a consequence of the fact that the contemporary far right is still often perceived as a twenty-first-century version of twentieth-century fascism. Fascism is based on the *Führerprinzip* (leadership principle) – where the leader is the personification of the party, the people, and the state – and much literature on fascism explains its support almost exclusively through the charismatic leader, an exceptional human being who commands the quasi-religious support of a devoted following.

This is very much at odds with the mainstream understanding of postwar democratic politics, in which political organizations, notably political parties, are seen as the key political actors. It is organizations, rather than individuals, that dominate democratic politics. That is not to say that individual leaders like Angela Merkel or Justin Trudeau do not play a role, but they function within the relatively tight constraints of an institutional political context, most notably their own political parties.

It is true that the far right has known many remarkable political leaders: both of radical right parties, like Jean-Marie Le Pen (FN) and Jörg Haider (FPÖ), and of extreme right organizations, like Michael Kühnen (ANS/NA) or Ian Stuart Donaldson (B&H). These leaders personify the organization, at least in the media, adding a personal story to the more abstract political ideology and organization. But for all the media attention that these mediagenic leaders generate, and the speculation about "*l'effect Le Pen*" (the Le Pen effect) and "*Führerparteien*" (leader parties), in most cases parties trump leaders.

Research shows that while leaders can pull in new supporters, they mostly either leave or become supporters of the organization, so that when the two go different ways, the vast majority stay loyal to the organization. This was most perfectly illustrated in Austria in 2005 when Jörg Haider, the allegedly charismatic leader of the FPO, decided to split from "his" party, but the vast majority of voters chose party over leader. In the parliamentary elections the following year, the FPÖ received 11 percent of the vote, while Haider's new Alliance for the Future of Austria gained only 4 percent.

Individual leaders play a more dominant role in many far-right groupuscules, like skinhead groups or neo-Nazi *Kameradschaften* (Comradeships). After all, here the formal organization is minimal and the group is not much more than the sum of the individuals. Local groups especially are often based primarily on the activism and charisma of one or a few men or women. Sometimes this becomes painfully clear: for example, when the leader moves to another area and the old group disappears but a new group emerges in the leader's new town. Still, even in smaller groups that are not locally based, leaders are much less dominant than received wisdom holds. Supporters come and go when leaders stay, and supporters stay when leaders go. In the end, most far-right activists in smaller groups are looking for a community and camaraderie, based around a provocative ideology, not a charismatic leader or surrogate father.

The Breeding Ground

During most of the first three waves of the postwar far right, the general assumption was that there was little demand for far-right politics. After all, it was, implicitly or explicitly, linked to historical fascism and the destruction of the Second World War. Much of the academic research on the postwar far right was based on this assumption, which two German social scientists termed the "normal pathology thesis" in an influential, if somewhat obscure, 1967 publication.[1] The thesis holds that only small parts of the population in western democracies support far-right ideas under normal conditions and that this only increases dramatically during times of crisis. This 5 to 10 percent of the population constitute a so-called "normal pathology," a relatively stable and constant presence of people who are ideologically unconnected to the political mainstream.

At least until the early 1990s, the normal pathology thesis seemed to be confirmed by the lack of mass support for far-right parties and politicians across Western Europe and North America. This led to an almost exclusive focus on the so-called demand side of far-right politics. The main question that drove the academic and public debate was: why would anyone support the far right? But as populist radical right parties started to gain significant electoral support in some European countries in the late 1990s, the thesis started to show its limitations. The focus shifted more to the supply side of far-right politics, and a new research question emerged: what kind of far right party is successful?

Simply stated, while the extreme right is indeed a normal pathology, largely unconnected to the political mainstream, the populist radical right is better seen as a pathological normalcy: that is, a radicalization of the political mainstream.[2] Extreme right groups tend to have a niche audience, as anti-democratic, antisemitic, and racist ideas are not just outside of the mainstream, they are rejected by vast majorities of the population in most countries. Moreover, in many countries, fascism is seen as the definition of evil, which means that any group or ideology that is related to it, let alone relates itself to it, is considered unacceptable. Consequently, few extreme right parties are electorally successful – although recent successes in some European countries, like Greece and Slovakia, seem to indicate that this is changing, as memories of the Second World War fade. At the same time, most openly (neo-)fascist groups recruit from a narrow part of the population, mostly lower educated, young men, who are attracted by the outsider and violent image of the far right.

In sharp contrast, most, if not all, countries have a fertile breeding ground for populist radical right ideas and organizations. Nativist, authoritarian, and populist attitudes are widespread, with often pluralities, and sometimes even majorities, expressing support for key populist radical right policies like less immigration, tougher sentences, and fewer perks for politicians. This is not to say that populist radical right values are identical to mainstream values or are shared by the majority of the populations. Rather, the radical right is a *radicalization* of the political mainstream, whose program is, in slightly more moderate form, supported by large sections of the population – and, in the fourth wave, growing sections of the political mainstream (see the next chapter).

Populist radical right values are disproportionately supported by specific subsets of the populations, particularly lower educated, working-class males from the majority "ethnic" or "racial" group. However, because of the postindustrial revolution and mass immigration, these groups are becoming a smaller part of the population in most western democracies. At the same time, younger generations, as well as minorities, are much more accepting of diversity, which could become a problem for future mobilization of the far right. Still, most populist radical right parties mobilize only a (small) part of their potential electorates. The reasons for this have to do with the supply side of politics: that is, the political context in which populist radical right parties mobilize and the product that they offer. However, all of this plays out within the context of a seemingly almighty media.

The Role of the Media

The media are both friend *and* foe of the far right. This can be explained, in part, by the ambiguity and hetero-geneity of the media. The media *are* rather than *is*, in the sense that they entail a broad plethora of individuals and institutions, which share very different goals and ideologies. Clearly, Fox News and the *New York Times* do not share many objectives, except, perhaps, making a profit. It is this overarching goal of the media which explains much of the ambiguous position of most media outlets towards the far right.

On the one hand, most media are not far right, and many even consider the far right a danger to democracy. On the other hand, they know that the far right sells. A picture or video of a group of skinheads with Nazi tattoos is therefore considered too good to waste. Editors know it will attract "eyeballs," which means revenue, and will therefore make it into a story. But because stories need to be "newsworthy," they often inflate the importance of the far right. A small group of fairly isolated and marginalized neo-Nazis become "a symptom" of a deeper societal phenomenon.

At the same time, mediagenic far-right politicians like Jair Bolsonaro, Nigel Farage, or Donald Trump have been endlessly interviewed, even at points in their careers when they were (still) marginal in the polls, because media know they provide spectacle. To justify the exposure, journalists will often be overly critical, and even combative, arguing that they "hold them to account." What happens, however, is not just that readers and viewers are exposed to their ideas, but that some will sympathize with the "underdog" far-right politician who is "unfairly attacked" by the "arrogant elite."

The fourth wave is characterized by the mainstreaming and normalization of the far right, which is particularly visible in the media. More and more mainstream media not only push the agenda of the radical right, but also are increasingly open and supportive of radical right politicians and parties. For all purposes, the British *Daily Express* was the unofficial newspaper of UKIP between 2013 and 2018, while Fox News has largely functioned as Trump's media cheerleader since he came to power in January 2017. But even "high-quality" media have changed tune significantly, normalizing populist radical right and Islamophobic politicians by employing them as columnists and occasional op-ed writers or through the presentation of them in sympathetic articles and soft-ball interviews. This is most notable in conservative media, like *Elsevier* in the Netherlands or *The Spectator* in the UK, but also in liberal media, like *de Volkskrant* in the Netherlands or the *New York Times* in the US. The most extreme example, however, is the opinion page of the *Wall Street Journal*, which regularly publishes far-right politicians (like Geert Wilders) and even officially endorsed Bolsonaro in the 2018 presidential elections.

There is a lot of debate on how influential *the* media are in politics. Decades of research shows that most people barely follow the news, and those who do are not easily swayed. In short, media coverage does not so much change issue positions, but it does determine which issues voters deem important. In this agenda-setting role, the media are increasingly supporting the populist radical right, by adopting its frames and issues as well as its voices. When the media almost exclusively focus on issues like crime, corruption, immigration, and terrorism – at the expense of, for instance, education, housing, and welfare – populist radical right policies and parties are indirectly made more relevant. This happened, for example, in the 2017 German parliamentary elections, when the AfD bounced back in the polls after the mainstream media focused on the one televised debate between the Christian Democrat leader Angela Merkel and the Social Democrat leader Manfred Schulz on Turkey, terrorism and internal security, and Islam.

However, media mainstreaming can also hurt the electoral support of populist radical right parties. As "populist radical right issues" dominate the public agenda, and media present their frames as "common sense," mainstream parties will start to adopt populist radical right positions, albeit in (slightly) more moderate form, which could keep voters from jumping ship or even have some radical right voters move (or return) to the mainstream right. What is essential here is whether the populist radical right *owns* the issue. Issue ownership means that voters associate a certain issue position with a particular party. If a populist radical right party owns the issue of opposition to European integration or immigration in a country, increased salience for these issues will benefit them. If they do not, other parties could profit (too).

The fourth wave of the postwar far right coincides with the ascendance of social media, which is often said to have changed the world forever. Not a major political event goes by without people claiming that social media caused it: from the Arab Spring to Trump's election victory. In fact, Trump's election is a good example of how social media really works. While his phenomenal Twitter following helped him get his message out, Trump had acquired his following because of his prominence in the traditional media – most notably his show *The Apprentice* on one of the three major national TV channels – and his social messages were brought into the living room of the average American by traditional media, including CNN and the *New York Times*.

Social media does play an important role for the far right, because it provides an opportunity to circumvent traditional media gatekeepers and push your way into the public debate. Many far-right parties and politicians have recognized the disruptive opportunities of social media, and mastered, or even pioneered, certain outlets and techniques. For example, Heinz-Cristian Strache (FPÖ) has used Facebook much more effectively than any other Austrian politician, while Geert Wilders (PVV), at least initially, and Matteo Salvini (League), have been highly effective on Twitter. Smaller far-right groups like CasaPound Italy and the Identitarians have been disproportionately effective on social media, undoubtedly helped by the fact that several of their leaders work(ed) in advertisement and communication.

However, the reach of social media remains mostly limited to the converted, or curious, without amplification by mainstream media. Given that many journalists live on Twitter, and some mistake their timeline for a representative sample of the real world, savvy far-right social media operators, from Matteo Salvini to Richard Spencer, have been able to reach a much bigger audience than their own followers.

Social media plays the biggest role for subcultures, some of which exist almost exclusively on the Internet. This is the case, first and foremost, for the "alt-right" (extreme right) and "alt-lite" (radical right), which are predominantly US-based, but have a broad international following and impact. The Internet allows isolated individuals to engage with each other and feel part of a bigger movement, often without having to face pushback for their far-right ideas, because they can operate anonymously and within homogenous social media bubbles. Moreover, these bubbles also function as echo chambers, which amplify the reach and intensity of the message, attracting some new followers and radicalizing old ones.

In the end, the relationship between the media and the far right is complex but changing. The media have always been both friend and foe to the far right. But whereas almost no significant media organizations were sympathetic to the far right during the third wave, several major right-wing media outlets are now closely associated with it: most notably Fox News and President Trump. Moreover, the far right has been normalized in many other media, including liberal newspapers. While social media has played a role, by further eroding the traditional media gatekeeper function, it has been more important for smaller and more marginal extreme (or "alt") right groups and subcultures than for bigger and successful populist radical right parties.

7

Consequences

In a 2012 lecture entitled "Three Decades of Populist Radical Right Parties in Western Europe: So What?," I concluded that the populist radical right was a "relatively minor nuisance" to liberal democracy in Western Europe and that the main challenge (still) came from the political mainstream. Moreover, I argued that "even in the unlikely event that PRRPs [populist radical right parties] become major players in West European politics, it is unlikely that this will lead to a fundamental transformation of the political system."[1] While I believe this conclusion still largely holds, I foresaw neither the extent of the political mainstreaming of the populist radical right nor the transformation of some of this "political mainstream" into full-fledged populist radical right parties.

A Question of Power

The consequences of far-right politics depend not only on the power of the far right (i.e. whether it is in government by itself, in coalition with non-far-right actors, or in opposition) but also on the political context within which it operates. Consolidated liberal democracies (like the UK and US) can potentially be impacted most, as they constitute the antithesis of the far right, but they might also prove more resilient to the far-right challenge. In contrast, less consolidated liberal democracies (like Brazil, India, and Israel) might change less, but more easily and quickly. While *direct* impact is somewhat easier to determine, most far-right groups primarily have *indirect* impact: that is, working through mainstream media and politics to achieve their goals.

Far-Right Governments

Until the beginning of the twenty-first century, the far right had only been in power in non-democracies like Franco's Spain or Pinochet's Chile, or replaced very young and fragile democracies like Weimar Germany or postcommunist Croatia. In this century, we see a growing number of populist radical right leaders and parties coming to power in more or less consolidated liberal democracies, such as Brazil, Hungary, and Poland. In most of these cases, however, the populist radical right status of these parties is debated, in academia and society, as they used to be (considered) mainstream right-wing parties.

When the populist radical right comes to power in a liberal democracy, it tries to move the country in an illiberal direction, undermining the independence of courts and the media, snubbing minority rights, and weakening the separation of powers. The level of success and control depends primarily on the strength of the populist radical right party and the complexity of the political system. Helped by a constitutional majority and a simple political system, for instance, Fidesz has encountered little opposition in establishing its "illiberal state" (see vignette 4 below), whereas PiS faces a bigger challenge, lacking a constitutional majority and operating in a more complex political system.

But the illiberal democracy populist radical right parties try to establish is of a special kind, namely an ethnocracy, a nominally democratic regime in which the dominance of one ethnic group is structurally determined. In the most extreme form, an ethnocracy would mean the expulsion of all "aliens," but only some extreme right groups openly support this. The FN laid out the blueprint of its preferred ethnocracy in its infamous Fifty-Point Program of 1991 – elaborated upon by VB leader Filip Dewinter in his Seventy-Point Program a year later – which included, among other things, a "national preference" for "native" French, segregated welfare states for "natives" and "aliens," and the rejection of religious rights for Islam and Muslims. In short, it would create a multi-ethnic France in which "non-natives," including immigrants and French citizens, would be reduced to second-class residents.

The most infamous case of an ethnocracy was undoubtedly Apartheid South Africa; incidentally, a regime that found great support within the global far right and whose demise is often bemoaned. More recently, in July 2018, Israel officially declared its state an ethnocracy, as its parliament – dominated by a coalition of radical right parties – passed the Nation-State Law, which enshrines Israel as "the national home of the Jewish people." Despite pressure from Hindutva extremists, the BJP-led National Democratic Alliance government has so far not officially defined India as "Hindustan," that is, a nation of Hindus, even though many prominent members see the country that way.

The illiberal pressures of far-right governments change not only the polity, but also everything and everyone within it. Other parties are forced to choose whether to collaborate with or oppose the government, which determines whether they get the carrot or the stick. Parties that collaborate run the risk of becoming coopted – like various regional parties within the BJP-dominated National Democratic Alliance – while those that oppose face increasing state pressure and repression. One of the most remarkable effects has been seen in Hungary, where the original far-right party, Jobbik, has rebranded itself as a mainstream party in light of Fidesz's radical right turn.

Far-Right Coalitions

It is rare that the far right is in power by itself, but populist radical right parties are more and more often part of broader coalition governments. In some cases, the populist radical right dominates the coalition, as in India, and possibly in Israel, where an increasingly radical right Likud has long governed coalitions with (other) radical right parties. To a certain extent, one could consider the Trump administration a radical right-dominated coalition, given that it includes both radical and mainstream right members and depends on Congressional support from the equally divided Republican Party. Similarly, in Brazil, President Bolsonaro has to govern without a majority in parliament as his own Social Liberal Party commands only a minority of seats in both houses.

In most cases, the radical right party is the junior partner in the coalition, while the senior partner delivers the premier and dominates the government. The senior partner is often an established liberal democratic party – such as the right-wing Austrian People's Party or the left-wing Bulgarian Socialist Party – but can also be a new, populist (but not far-right) upstart – like Forza

Italia or the Five Star Movement in Italy. In general, coalition governments primarily reflect the policies and priorities of the senior party, and coalitions with populist radical right parties are no exception to this rule. That said, the senior partner has often moved more towards the junior party in the run-up to the government formation, which means that "its" policies and priorities are, at least in part, those of the populist radical right. Moreover, these governments are coalitions, which means that compromises have to be made and that even the senior party has to accept some power-sharing and scrutiny from other power holders. Ultimately, while these governments do show illiberal, and particularly nativist, impulses, most of the more radical policies are either watered down in the national government or parliament, and sometimes at the federal or local level, or shot down by the courts. One can see this clearly in the US, where President Trump has experienced serious opposition from Congressional Republicans, as well as independent judges, with regard to his controversial "Muslim ban" or "Voter Fraud Commission."

In some cases, populist radical right parties have been the support party of a minority government, which means that they enter into an agreement with the government party/ies to provide them with majority support in parliament. In exchange, they tend to get prominent positions within parliament, for example chairmanships of important committees, as well as policy concessions. Sometimes, far-right parties can have at least as much influence as a support party than as an official coalition party. The best example of this is the DF, which supported a series of right-wing minority governments in Denmark (2001–11, 2016–19), significantly tightening immigration law and strengthening integration requirements.

Far-Right Oppositions

Most opposition parties have only limited policy power, given that government parties make the vast majority of laws. However, they can, and do, set the political agenda, determining what issues are discussed and how they are framed. This is particularly the case for far-right parties that have a significant parliamentary representation. As party systems have fragmented, and far-right parties have increased their success, many countries have much larger coalitions these days, which sometimes include all major mainstream parties, leaving the far right as the largest opposition party in the country (e.g. the AfD in Germany).

There is no doubt that the far right is increasingly successful in agenda-setting, often (unintentionally) helped by opportunistic mainstream politicians and sensationalist mainstream media. In many European countries, it has been able to keep the "immigration" issue at the top of the agenda, while framing it as a threat and integration as a problem. Similarly, European integration is now almost universally discussed as having gone too far, requiring the return of national compe-tencies, and terms like "establishment" and "elite" have largely become disqualifiers.

Until recently, far-right opposition parties mainly affected the discourse of mainstream parties, and to some extent governments. Given that the content of the policies did not change that much, a growing gap between discourse and policies emerged, which only furthered political dissatisfaction and support for populist radical right parties and policies. This is in part what led to the victory of Donald Trump in the Republican primaries – a man who said he would really do what the other Republicans had only talked about doing.

Domestic Consequences

I will assess the political impact of the far right on both national and international politics. With regard to the domestic consequences of far-right politics, I will discuss the impact first on the people (notably public opinion), then on policies, and finally on polities (i.e. the political systems). In the next chapter, on "responses," the specific consequences for other political parties will be addressed. In vignette 4, the specific case of Viktor Orbán's Hungary will be analyzed, the first example of a populist radical right state in the twenty-first century, and increasingly the model of far-right actors across Europe (and beyond).

The People

Virtually all far-right groups aim to influence public opinion, although for a broad variety of goals and through a broad variety of means. Where some neo-Nazi skins use music to attract supporters and violence to intimidate opponents, populist radical right parties focus more on elections and policies to achieve similar aims. Extreme right groups tend to have relatively little success in winning people over to their openly racist and undemocratic ideas, but their violence can have a chilling effect on the population, especially on groups targeted by them. Particularly in some East European towns and cities, extreme right groups have terrorized "alien" populations to create what East German neo-Nazis call *national befreite Zone* (nationally liberated zones), that is, areas "cleansed" of (perceived) immigrants and other ethnic minorities (such as Roma).

As targeted groups feel less safe in the public space, they will also become more critical towards key political and state institutions, from parliament to police. The targeted populations often already have significant distrust of state agencies, particularly law enforcement (because of discrimination and violence), which means they won't report incidents or ask for protection. Often, they believe police officers sympathize with far-right groups too. This is not without reason. In many countries (e.g. France and Greece), police officers disproportionately support populist radical right parties and, particularly at the local level, personal connections with far-right groups and individuals are tight.

But growing support for populist radical right parties will have a similar effect on targeted populations, who will start to perceive significant parts of both society and the state as hostile to their interests, if not their outright presence. This will be even stronger when populist radical right parties are mainstreamed and normalized in broader society, let alone when they participate in (national and local) governments. In the end, this could lead these targeted populations to lose trust in the whole political system.

The relationship between public opinion of the general population and populist radical right parties is more complex than is often assumed. Public opinion is both a cause and consequence of their electoral success, although there is much stronger evidence for the former than the latter. Most populist radical right parties achieve their electoral breakthrough from the political margins, being almost absent from the mainstream media. Given that their ideology is closely related to mainstream values, rather than fundamentally opposed to them (see chapter 6), they do not have to change people's minds. What they need is for the public debate to shift to their topics, and use their frames, which often happens without the populist radical right playing a major role in the process.

Still, there is little empirical evidence that this all significantly influences public opinion. While surveys show an increase in anti-establishment sentiments and Euroscepticism in much of Europe, anti-immigrant sentiments were already high – even in countries that had little immigration before 2015 – and seem to be slightly decreasing in Western Europe, as younger people become more comfortable with diversity. Similarly, in the US, opposition to immigration has been declining since (at least) 1995, while support for immigration has been rising, and Trump's presidency has done nothing to stop this. Within the EU, we even see some signs of a liberal democratic backlash to far-right success. For example, support for the EU has gone (back) up after Brexit, and is particularly high in Hungary and Poland, despite, or maybe because of, deeply Eurosceptic populist radical right governments.

The biggest effect is not on issue positions but on issue salience: that is, how important people think an issue is – and perhaps also on the intensity of their position. This is a direct consequence of the emphasis put on issues in the media, which is again related to choices by both mainstream and radical right politicians. Overall, however, the far right's effect on public opinion is mostly indirect, through agenda-setting, and largely dependent upon the political mainstream (media and politics) adopting its issues and frames uncritically. For instance, the EU-wide Eurobarometer surveys have shown for years the high salience of issues like immigration and terrorism, even in countries where both phenomena are minor to non-existent.

The Policies

Despite the fact that the populist radical right has set the political agenda in many European countries during most of the twenty-first century so far, words have spoken louder than actions for much of the time. Mainstream parties of the right *and* left have moved significantly to the right in terms of their discourse on corruption, crime, European integration, and immigration, but made mainly cosmetic policy changes. For instance, while British prime minister David Cameron and French president Nicolas Sarkozy declared multiculturalism a failure, they toughened some integration criteria and demands, but did not fundamentally change immigration or integration policies. Similarly, while many North European prime ministers criticized the EU for being too powerful and out of touch, and promised to oppose a next bailout, they did not provide clear alternative European futures and, inevitably, supported future bailouts. The political scientist Antonis Ellinas has called this strategy "to play and then retract the nationalist card."[2]

The so-called "refugee crisis," in combination with a spike in jihadist terrorism in Western Europe, has quickly closed the gap between discourse and policy. In response to German chancellor Angela Merkel's *Willkommenspolitik* ("Welcome Politics") in 2015, opening Germany and thereby much of the EU to asylum seekers, Hungarian prime minister Viktor Orbán led a nativist backlash of a growing coalition of member states. Central and East European countries were the most overt and vocal in their opposition to non-European immigration, and most radical in their new anti-immigration policies – including the building of fences and the criminalization of undocumented immigrants – but many West European governments were happy to follow their lead. Several of the most strident anti-immigrant governments are dominated by the populist radical right (e.g. Hungary, Poland), but others are not (e.g. Austria, Denmark, Slovakia), and some even officially exclude populist radical right parties from the government (e.g. the Czech Republic, the Netherlands).

Outside of Europe, radical right parties and politicians have also mainly affected counter-terrorism and immigration policies. President Trump has finally passed his "Muslim ban," albeit in moderated form and after significant judicial and political opposition; continues his pressure to build a (larger) wall at the southern border with Mexico; and even plans a significant overhaul of legal immigration, which would prioritize European immigrants. Israel has become even less open to asylum seekers, and has adopted the Nation-State Law, which further marginalizes Arab Israelis. And while the BJP-led Indian government has mainly focused on (neoliberal) economic policies, it did try to pass a nationwide "beef ban," playing to Hindu nationalist and Islamophobic sentiments, which was struck down by the Supreme Court in 2017. In addition, with regard to the millions of "illegal immigrants" in India's northeast, the government has said that Hindu migrants from Bangladesh should be protected, but Muslims who are found to be illegal should be expelled.

The Polities

Until recently, far-right parties did not affect their respective polities either, at least not in more fundamental terms. Studies showed that while governments with populist radical right participation tried to undermine independent courts or media, and abolish minority rights (notably for Muslims), they were generally opposed by coalition partners, civil society organizations, and independent courts. Given that they lacked a parliamentary majority, let alone a constitutional one, they would be dependent upon coalition partners, which either did not share their objectives, or feared the populist radical right would abuse their new powers. So, while independent courts and media would be criticized, and immigrant and minority rights would be weakened, this would not be much different from other right-wing governments in surrounding countries. The situation has changed in recent years, particularly in certain Central and East European countries (such as Hungary and Poland), but also in India, Israel, and the US. The main challenges come primarily from conservative-turned-populist radical right parties and politicians. Ever since he entered the White House, President Trump has relentlessly criticized journalists and judges who oppose him, suggesting new measures to curtail their independence. But, to date, he has tried to change his political environment primarily by replacing the personnel rather than the institutional structure. In Poland, the new populist radical right government has mounted a frontal attack on the courts and media, but has been resisted by civil society, judges, opposition parties, and the international community. PiS is trying to follow the "Budapest model," but lacks Orbán's constitutional majority and, so far, staying power. What a populist radical right government looks like we can see in Hungary, which Orbán has transformed from a liberal democracy into a competitive authoritarian regime, devoid of independent courts and media, as well as free and fair elections (see vignette 4).

International Consequences

A think tank report on "the populist challenge to foreign policy," of which I was a co-author, concluded only a few years ago that "Europe's troublemakers" had only modest influence on foreign policy and the international community.[3] Adding insult to injury, it was published just a few months before a majority of Brits decided to leave the EU, undoubtedly one of the most important foreign policy decisions in Europe in the twenty-first century. While the EU referendum was primarily a consequence of internal divisions within the Conservative Party, UKIP's electoral competition played a role in David Cameron's call for an EU referendum, and UKIP's anti-immigrant campaign played a major role in making Brexit a reality.

Although the Brexit vote was a major foreign policy success for the far right, the consequent incompetence and infighting over the type of Brexit and post-Brexit world desired are emblematic of the foreign policy divisions within the far right. In sharp contrast to the sensationalist media narratives about a nationalist international, far-right groups are fundamentally divided over the most basic foreign policy issues. What brings them together, by and large, is a disdain for the current global order, defined by cultural, economic, and political integration (even if more in theory than practice).

Consequently, European populist radical right parties, and (coalition) governments, are increasingly able to frustrate international collaboration, like the UN's Intergovernmental Conference on the Global Compact for Immigration in Marrakesh (2018), and sometimes even block it, like the EU refugee resettlement plan (2017), but they cannot fundamentally change it, let alone create an alternative global order. This will probably not change after the 2019 European elections, even when a new populist radical right Eurosceptic super-group emerges, because the individual parties always put national over European interests. And their national interests, both inside and outside of the EU, differ significantly, and often oppose each other: for instance, some are from countries that are net payers to the EU (e.g. the FPÖ and FvD), while others are from net receivers (e.g. Fidesz and Vox).

Even President Trump has mainly limited the US role in international organizations and treaties, including

NATO and the UN, rather than seeking to abolish or transform them. And in the few cases where he has withdrawn the US, such as from the Paris Agreement on Climate Change (2017) or the UN Human Rights Council (2018), this has been supported by neoconservatives as much as by the radical right in the Republican Party. Trump has also repeatedly disappointed foreign far-right allies by lukewarm support, and sometimes even critique, of their own pet projects – from Brexit to Greater Israel. In fact, in response to Trump's erratic "America First" foreign policy, support for closer cooperation within the EU and NATO has increased rather than decreased, to the dismay of much of the European far right.

Vignette 4: Orbán's Hungary

Helped by corruption scandals in the Socialist government, and division and infighting within the liberal democratic camp, Viktor Orbán returned to power with a massive victory in the 2010 elections. During its eight years of opposition, Fidesz had created a parallel society and state, sustained by a myriad of "civic circles" (*Polgari Körök*) and partisan media. Despite radical, and at times even violent, opposition to the Socialist government, Fidesz had campaigned on a relatively vague, national conservative agenda. But emboldened by an unexpected constitutional majority, Orbán wasted little time in implementing a program that has transformed Hungary from a liberal democracy into an "illiberal state."

Orbán has reduced parliament to a partisan rubber-stamping institution, which does little else than uncritically introduce and pass

Viktor Orbán speaks at the European People's Party congress in Bucharest, Romania, in 2012.
(Source: European People's Party/Flickr/2012.)

government-initiated legislation. He has weakened non-majoritarian institutions, from courts to tax offices, by limiting their power and stacking them with cronies. He has criticized independent civil society organizations and media, frustrating their operations by new legislation and withdrawal of state funding. A network of businessmen associated with Fidesz, and more specifically Orbán himself, started to buy up most of the Hungarian media, folding some (including the well-regarded newspaper *Népszabadszág*) and eventually consolidating the others and donating them to an "independent" national foundation, run by a loyalist. Today, with the exception of one TV station (RTL Klub) and a few websites, the Hungarian media are completely under Orbán's control.

While Orbán had largely stayed out of major international debates in his first term after returning to power, he has become a major European player in the wake of the "refugee crisis," successfully taking on Angela Merkel and blocking the EU's proposed refugee redistribution plan. Now openly embracing populist radical right positions, Orbán has transformed Hungary into an illiberal democracy, using nativist campaigns against asylum seekers to marginalize his remaining political opponent, Jobbik, while intensifying an antisemitic campaign against the Jewish US-Hungarian philanthropist George Soros to curtail civil society and drive out the Central European University. With his recent move to create a parallel, partisan judiciary, overpowering the nominally independent judiciary, Hungary is no longer liberal or democratic. It has become a competitive authoritarian state, which allows an increasingly embattled and harassed opposition to exist only on the political margins.

The fact that Hungary could transform from a liberal democratic into a far-right authoritarian regime within the EU, which was founded to prevent the emergence of exactly such regimes, is a painful illustration of politics in the fourth wave. First, it shows the transformation of a mainstream right-wing party into a populist radical right one. Second, rather than meeting broad opposition from the European political mainstream, as would have happened during the third wave, Fidesz was protected by the mainstream right European People's Party, the main political group in the European Parliament. Third, while Orbán is a loud and open Eurosceptic, his approach to the EU is offensive rather than defensive. He does not want to leave the EU; he wants to transform it in Hungary's image.

8

Responses

I rarely give a public lecture where I am not asked the question, "What can we do to defeat the far right?" Understandably, many people are not so much interested in the various actions, ideologies, and organizations of the far right, but are mainly concerned about its negative impact on liberal democracy, and the perceived incompetence, and unwillingness, of mainstream parties to deal with it. I share this interest, both as an academic and as a citizen, but have to admit that, even after more than two decades, I still do not have the answer.

Around the world, countries approach the far right, and political extremism more generally, in different ways, depending on a broad range of factors, such as the country's history, the strength of the liberal democratic system, and the perceived threat of the far-right challenge. This chapter will discuss the key responses by the state, political parties, and civil society. It ends with a short discussion of the crucial question: do they work?

The State: Between the German and the US Models

The essence of a liberal democratic system is not just majority rule, but also the protection of minority rights. While today the term "minority" is mainly associated with "ethnic" or "racial" groups, in legal terms it extends to a much broader range of categories, including political minorities. However, not every state tolerates political minorities to the same extent. With regard to the far right, the distinction between the German and the US models is the most relevant.

Although the US has a long history of far-right politics, including a toxic mix of authoritarianism and racism, these are mostly associated with mainstream, and so supposedly democratic, parties. Fascist and quasi-fascist movements and personalities – such as the German American Bund and Father Charles Coughlin – were quite popular in the early twentieth century, but were seen as "imported" and "Un-American." And except for the attack on Pearl Harbor, the country remained free from fascist(-linked) territorial destruction, let alone occupation.

This specific historical context explains in part why the US has remained so tolerant to the far right, which, like all other political groups, is protected by the iron-clad First Amendment of the US Constitution: "Congress shall make no law respecting an estab-lishment of religion, or prohibiting the free exercise thereof; or abridging the freedom of speech, or of the press; or the right of the people peaceably to assemble, and to petition the Government for a redress of griev-ances." Freedom of speech is sacrosanct in the US, at least it has been since the late 1960s, and protects even the most extreme organizations and speech. The most famous example of this is the so-called "Skokie

Affair" of 1977, when the National Socialist Party of America wanted to march through Skokie, Illinois, a Chicago suburb with a particularly large number of Jewish inhabitants, including Holocaust survivors. The American Civil Liberties Union challenged the village's ban on the march, and the use of Nazi uniforms and swastikas, arguing it infringed on the party's First Amendment rights. In the end, the Supreme Court ruled in agreement with the American Civil Liberties Union and the National Socialist Party of America.

This stands in sharp contrast with the Federal Republic of Germany, which was built as a direct response to the Weimar Republic, which was considered, in hindsight, too tolerant to survive a significant (right-wing) extremist challenge. Consequently, the new postwar German state was constructed to prevent the far right from ever coming to power by democratic means again. The Federal Republic is a so-called *wehrhafte Demokratie* (militant democracy), in which the main political institutions (executive, legislature, and judiciary) are given extensive powers and duties to defend the liberal democratic orders.

Most importantly, social groups that are deemed "hostile" to the liberal democratic order can be banned by the interior minister – although they can appeal the decision in court – while "hostile" political parties can be banned (only) by the fiercely independent Federal Constitutional Court. Consequently, hundreds of extreme right groups have been banned, often small neo-Nazi *Kameradschaften*, but only one extreme right party, the Socialist Reich Party, in 1952. The NPD has been threatened by a party ban for most of its (long) existence. It survived a first court case in 2001–3, when the Federal Constitutional Court dismissed the case because the party was so full of informants and infiltrators that the Court could not accurately distinguish between the party and the state.

In another attempt, a few years later, the Court did declare the party "hostile to the Constitution" and urged parliament to starve it of public funds, but also refused to ban it. Importantly, the differences between the German and the US models exclude the use of violence. In all countries, including the US, the state monitors potentially violent groups, including on the far right. However, across the globe, anti-racist activists and left-wing politicians have long complained that the state, and particularly intelligence and law enforcement services, are "blind on the right eye": that is, they ignore or minimize the threat from far-right violence. Since the terrorist attacks of 9/11, many states have refocused their priorities, and thereby resources, on jihadi terrorism, often to the detriment of investigating far-right terrorism. For instance, in the Netherlands, only one person within the Dutch General Intelligence and Security Service remained responsible for "extremism" (including the far right) post-9/11.

The situation in the US is particularly disturbing in this respect. In the wake of the 9/11 attacks, the newly created Department of Homeland Security had forty analysts for jihadi terrorism and a mere six for "domestic non-Islamic terrorism," which includes left-wing terrorism and so-called "ecoterrorism" too. When the Department published a report on "right-wing terrorism" in 2009, in which it warned against possible terrorist attacks by military veterans (like the man who was responsible for the Oklahoma City bombing in 1995), the conservative backlash was so fierce that Homeland Security Secretary Janet Napolitano offered an official apology. The next year, the team responsible for the report was dissolved and the major analyst left in frustration, claiming only two members were left analyzing the far right. Despite the increase in far-right violence in the US, which has been more deadly and regular than jihadi terrorism since 9/11, the situation has continued to deteriorate. In recent years, the Trump presidency has withdrawn funding from several anti-far-right violence initiatives and has used the term "terrorism" exclusively for (alleged) jihadist perpetrators.

The Parties: From Demarcation to Incorporation

As politics in most western democracies is first and foremost party politics, the question of how liberal democratic parties should deal with far-right parties is crucial to the broader question of how to respond to the far right. Among the myriad of different approaches, we can distinguish between four prominent and distinct ones: demarcation, confrontation, cooptation, and incorporation.[1]

Demarcation

Demarcation means that liberal democratic parties exclude far-right parties from their political interactions. They try to ignore them and continue with their day-to-day politics as if the far-right party (or parties) does not exist. For much of the postwar era, this was the de facto approach towards the various small radical right parties in all western democracies; although some (openly) extreme right parties and groups were banned, particularly in the first decade of the postwar era. Once populist radical right parties started to increase their electoral support, other parties were forced to take a more explicit, and formal, position. Most mainstream parties officially declared populist radical right parties to be outside of the democratic realm and therefore excluded them from the political game.

After yet another "Black Sunday," that is, an electoral victory of the radical right Flemish Bloc (later Flemish Interest, VB), all other parliamentary parties in Flanders, the Dutch-speaking northern part of Belgium, came together and formally agreed to constitute a so-called *cordon sanitaire* around the VB. Officially, the cordon had a fairly limited mandate: it excluded any political coalition, on whatever level of government, with the VB. Unofficially, it excluded not only the party, but also its main issue (immigration), and thereby the major concern of its voters. Despite ups and downs in the electoral successes of the VB, the *cordon sanitaire* has not been broken since its (second) introduction in 1992.

Political parties in many western democracies still practice demarcation today, though only Belgium has an official *cordon sanitaire*. The AfD is excluded in Germany, the RN in France, the PVV in the Netherlands (except for 2010–12), and the SD in Sweden. But in all these countries, for a variety of reasons, the unofficial cordons are starting to show cracks, with growing dissent particularly among local and regional politicians of mainstream right-wing parties. In the end, demarcation, be it official or not, is always more strategic than ideological. Whenever it becomes expedient for a specific party to break the cordon, it will, arguing it has outlived its purpose, because the populist radical right party is allegedly no longer outside of the liberal democratic order, or that it is undemocratic to marginalize certain voters.

Confrontation

A confrontation strategy entails an active opposition to far-right parties and, most often, their policies. This is mostly limited to very small or very extreme parties, such as the NPD in Germany and XA in Greece. They are mainly confronted on their most extreme positions – such as anti-democracy, antisemitism, historical revisionism, and racism – and are attacked for their (alleged) propensity for violence, whether through incitement or actual violent actions. These confrontations mainly have symbolic value, and are sometimes even shared by radical right parties, in an attempt to show that they are "moderate" and not far right. The most cynical example is Fidesz,' which regularly uses the specter of an "extreme right" Jobbik-dominated Hungary to silence domestic and, particularly, foreign critics of its own radical right policies.

While confrontations with small or extreme parties have overall low benefits, but also low costs, this is not so for confrontations with large or populist radical right parties. First of all, if the far-right party is big, it could be a potential coalition partner, or at least could be used as such in coalition negotiations with other parties. This applies especially to mainstream right parties, which are often facing a mainstream left party that does have acceptable left coalition partners: that is, Green and even some radical left parties. If center-right parties exclude far-right parties *a priori*, they weaken their own hand in the coalition negotiations with center-left parties.

Second, and more important, confrontations could push away potential voters, who are choosing between the mainstream and populist radical right, and even some of the mainstream's own voters. While few voters will be lost over opposition to anti-democratic or antisemitic positions, this is no longer the case with illiberal, and especially Islamophobic, positions. Hence, if a mainstream party confronts a populist radical right party over its anti-immigrant or anti-Islam agenda, it could be perceived as (too) pro-immigrant and pro-Islam by mainstream voters, including their own.

Not surprisingly, then, confrontation has become less and less common in the twenty-first century as populist radical right parties have become more successful electorally and more relevant politically. The main parties that continue to openly confront populist radical right parties are the Greens and some social liberal parties, like the Dutch Democrats 66 and the French "The Republic on the Move!" of President Emanuel Macron, which have little overlap in potential voters. If mainstream parties still confront populist radical right parties, they focus almost exclusively on the leaders, while acknowledging the "legitimate concerns" of their "misguided" voters, which brings us to the third strategy.

Cooptation

At least since the late 1990s, cooptation has become the dominant model of interaction in western democracies. This means that liberal democratic parties exclude populist radical right parties, but not their ideas. This is a logical consequence of the opportunistic confrontation strategy that many mainstream parties adopted when populist radical right parties increased their electoral support and political power. Cooptation exists in different forms and gradations. Almost all major European leaders have criticized "multiculturalism," including German chancellor Angela Merkel, who at the same time remains staunchly opposed to the normalization of the AfD (let alone the NPD). Similarly, more conservative politicians, like John Howard in Australia or Bart De Wever in Belgium, have made their career attacking their radical right opponents, while simultaneously adopting much of their program.

Initially, liberal democratic parties primarily adopted populist radical right discourse, problematizing

European integration and multiculturalism, without substantially changing their policies. The only real change in the late twentieth century was in terms of refugee policies as a consequence of populist radical right opposition to the sudden influx of refugees from the Yugoslav civil war in the early 1990s. In the early twenty-first century, the gap between discourse and policy grew wider, until several developments, most notably terrorist attacks and the so-called "refugee crisis" (often linked in both populist radical right and mainstream right discourses), led to a slew of authoritarian and nativist policies from mainstream governments (see chapter 7).

Incorporation

Incorporation means that not just populist radical right positions, but also populist radical right parties, are mainstreamed and normalized.[2] The first time this happened in postwar Europe was in 1994, in Italy, where right-wing populist Silvio Berlusconi created a coalition government with the "post-fascist" National Alliance and the populist radical right LN. The government came after a complete implosion of the existing party system and lasted only eight months, after which the LN pulled the plug.

In 2000, the FPÖ entered a coalition government with the conservative Austrian People's Party, which led to massive pushback in Austria and Europe. Egged on by the Austrian Social Democrats, which had negotiated in secret with FPÖ too, hundreds of thousands of Austrians took to the streets to demonstrate against the "fascist" government. The (then) fourteen other EU member states had tried to prevent the coalition with a strong statement, saying they would "not promote or accept any bilateral official contacts at a political level" with a government including the FPÖ. In the end, the EU-14 only boycotted the FPÖ ministers and appointed a committee of three "wise men," which recommended that the sanctions should be lifted. Despite mutterings from some EU member states, and the Austrian Social Democrats, the sanctions were lifted after less than a year. When the FPÖ returned to government in 2018, there were much smaller demonstrations in Austria, and no EU government boycotted FPÖ ministers. This time the FPÖ was able to get the coveted foreign minister position, but decided to appoint the independent former diplomat and political analyst Karin Kneissl to prevent international boycotts (only Israel boycotts her). It was an indication of the normalization of incorporation. Populist radical right parties have been in coalition governments in many different countries and supported minority govern-ments in several more.

The increasing incorporation of populist radical right parties is, both directly and indirectly, a result of their growing electoral relevance – and, at least as important, the public perception of their rise, which is inflated by sensationalist media accounts. On the one hand, populist radical right parties are now so big in many countries that excluding them from government creates increasingly high costs for particularly mainstream right-wing parties – that is, either Grand Coalitions with the main center-left party, which means sharing more power, or coalitions with two or three other parties, which tend to be more ideologically diverse and (therefore) less politically stable. On the other hand, many mainstream right-wing parties have been moving to the right for over a decade, particularly on socio-cultural issues, so that the populist radical right is increasingly its most logical coalition partner in terms of ideological fit.

Civil Society: Between Non-Violent and Violent Resistance

Beyond the state and political parties, civil society groups play a major role in responding to the rise of the far right. Where political parties increasingly prefer cooptation and incorporation, particularly in the fourth wave, this is much less the case for civil society organizations. Few religious or trade union organizations have coopted nativist or populist rhetoric, and even those that no longer exclude or confront far-right groups and individuals at best tolerate rather than incorporate them, accepting them but not their ideologies. Particularly in the public image, civil society is still primarily characterized by demarcation and confrontation.

Demarcation

Many civil society organizations bar their members from being active within far-right organizations or, at the very least, from being candidates for far-right parties or leaders of far-right groups. This has traditionally been the case for almost all trade unions, which have long been among the best organized and most vocal opponents of the far right. Union members who stood in elections for populist radical right parties would be expelled, while union leaders who expressed sympathy for populist radical right parties would be forced to choose between the union and the party. This applied to most Christian democratic and social democratic unions – and even more so for communist unions. As a consequence, some populist radical right parties tried to create their own trade unions, particularly within sectors that are known to be sympathetic to the far right. In the late 1990s, the FN created unions for police officers (FN-Police) and prison guards (FN-Pénitentiaire), but both were ruled unlawful by the French Supreme Court of Appeal. In countries where the far right is more mainstreamed, some trade unions are close or sympathetic to major far-right parties, like the Indian Workers' Union, the labor wing of the RSS, which has over 6 million members.

While most trade unions continue to officially oppose the far right in the fourth wave, there are significant national and sectoral differences. For example, in countries where the populist radical right has been mainstreamed, if not outright normalized, like Denmark, trade unions mainly try to ignore the elephant in the room. In countries where the populist radical right is not yet a serious player, however, like (until a few years ago) Germany and the US, trade unions are (or were) still resolute in their demarcation. However, even in the US, there are sectoral differences within the broader trade union movement, depending, to a large extent, on how widespread support for Donald Trump is within the specific union's membership.

Similarly, while far-right groups, both parties and social movement organizations, were excluded from cultural, political, and social events in most European countries during the third wave, particularly in the western part, this *cordon sanitaire* is rapidly breaking down and has even largely disappeared in some countries. For example, far-right publishers are now routinely represented at international and national book fairs after decades of exclusion, even though, like the Antaios stand of "new right" ideologue and publisher Goetz Kubitschek at the 2017 Frankfurt Book Fair, they are largely shunned.

Confrontation

Although tacit toleration, rather than open incorporation, is becoming more and more common during the fourth wave, confrontation remains an important part of civil society responses to the far right. Some of the largest demonstrations in recent years have been, directly or indirectly, against the far right, from the explicitly anti-racist demonstration in Berlin in 2018, attracting almost a quarter million of people, to the more implicitly anti-far-right Women's Marches across the US, mobilizing between 3 and 5 million people in 2017.

In addition to the occasional large anti-racist demonstrations, there are smaller but more regular "anti-fascist" demonstrations. While the former are often reactions to far-right events, but organized in a different space and time, the latter are direct confrontations with the far right. The various counter-demonstrations also have different goals, from showing the far right that they are not welcome in a town, or showing the broader public that the far right does not represent the majority, to preventing the far right from organizing and spreading its "message of hate."

As noted in chapter 5, most far-right demonstrations are confronted with much bigger anti-fascist counter-demonstrations. There are many pictures of "demonstrations" by a few dozen far-right activists surrounded by ten to twenty times as many anti-fascists, separated by an often massive police force. This has been the case for every hyped "alt-right" rally in the US, including the deadly "Unite the Right" rally in Charlottesville in 2017. But it is also the case for most demonstrations of the EDL and PEGIDA, and certainly their many unsuccessful local and international offshoots. For instance, even in Dresden, the only city where PEGIDA has at times mobilized tens of thousands of supporters, counter-demonstrators almost always matched if not exceeded its numbers.

Anti-fascists come in many different guises. The media image is that of a black-clad, young and violent, mostly male anarchist, who hates both "fascism" and "the state." This so-called "black bloc" is often only a small minority of larger counter-demonstrations, despite featuring prominently in media reports, but more significant among smaller counter-demonstrations, particularly against more violent extreme right groups. The "black bloc" resembles the fascists it battles in the streets in many ways, from demographics (young, male) to fashion (black hoodies, combat boots) to strategy (confrontational and violent). In some cases, the relationships between individual anti-fascists and fascists are so close that they have each other's phone numbers and communicate outside of demonstrations.

Anti-fascist demonstrations and demonstrators are generally not violent, although violence is more common on the margins of the demonstrations and the movement. It is this threat of violence that gives the anti-fascists, and particularly the "black bloc," such a high media profile. It consequently also transforms irrelevant far-right events, from invited speeches at universities to small local protests, into high-profile media events, as we have seen in the US in the past years (e.g. in Berkeley, California, and Portland, Oregon). This symbiotic relationship, as well as the spiral of (potential) violence associated with it, is a bone of contention within the broader anti-fascist and particularly anti-racist movement.

Do These Responses to the Far Right Work?

Which approach works best depends on a broad variety of objective and subjective conditions, including the history of a country, the political culture, the strength of both liberal democracy and the far-right group, and the control/role of the media. But, more than anything, it depends on what the key objective of the approach is. This is itself linked to what the understanding of (liberal) democracy is; more specifically, whether one believes that the intolerant should be tolerated.

If the key objective is to minimize the direct impact of far-right groups, nothing is more effective than a ban. An oft-heard argument against banning extreme right groups is that this would drive their members underground and into terrorism. While this argument is popular, the empirical evidence is so far inconclusive. Only a tiny portion of the population is willing to use violence to advance its political goals, and while this group might be somewhat bigger among members of the far right, it is still very small. Moreover, most far-right violence is more or less spontaneous, rather than premeditated, and far-right terrorists are not disgruntled former members of now banned groups or parties.

Banning far-right parties is also the best way to prevent them from winning votes, and consequently influencing other parties and potentially policies, presuming it is done before they achieve their electoral breakthrough. But banned parties can re-emerge in more moderate forms, at least in terms of their public image, without having changed their ideology. This was the case, for example, with the Flemish Bloc, which reinvented itself as Flemish Interest after a 2004 conviction had made its political functioning virtually impossible. Except for the name and party color, which changed from orange to yellow, the two VBs were near identical in terms of ideology and leadership. At least initially, the party even profited from the "ban" in electoral terms, although it might have led to its decline later on, when voters increasingly looked for alternatives that were more acceptable to other parties.

Moreover, where do we draw the line in terms of which ideas and organizations should be banned? While majorities might agree on the banning of openly neo-Nazi parties, contemporary populist radical right parties are much closer to the political mainstream, and therefore considered less, or not, problematic. And even if the French were to agree on banning a party like, say, Marine Le Pen's RN, on the basis of its nativist agenda, what would be the legal argument to not ban mainstream parties like the (French) Republicans, which have copied much of the discourse and policies of the Le Pens over the past decades?

Assuming we accept at least the right of populist radical right parties to exist legally, but we want to limit their electoral success and therefore political impact, which of the four approaches works best? In general, demarcation works best, but only under certain conditions. First and foremost, all major parties must engage in it. Second, the media must be supportive of it. And, third, the timing must be right. The populist radical right party must not be too big or important to coalition formation – because it can then lead to "anti-far-right" coalitions that are too large and ineffective. The key challenge of the *cordon sanitaire* is, however, to exclude far-right parties, but not their issues – which is different from their issue frames and positions.

In Belgium and Sweden, for example, the exclusion of the far-right party went hand in hand with rendering the issue of immigration almost taboo, despite real and perceived grievances within the population. This led to the eventual electoral breakthrough, and then continued growth, of the SD in Sweden, while other parties moved into the VB's territory in Flanders: first the right-wing populist List Dedecker and later the conservative, Flemish nationalist New Flemish Alliance. While it seemed that the cordon had at least continued to marginalize the VB, if no longer its issues and issue positions, its recent return indicates that this might just have been temporary.

Confrontation with radical right parties has rarely been used, at least not by the most important parties (i.e. the mainstream right and left), which compete with them electorally. If mainstream politicians attacked radical right leaders and parties, they mostly did this in combination with acceptance of their issue positions, albeit in somewhat more moderate form, or with their voters' "legitimate grievances." In other words, confrontation was really cooptation. Even the genuine confrontation of Green and social liberal parties did not necessarily harm the populist radical right, as it raised the salience of "their" issues and made them more central to the electoral campaign and political struggle. Collaboration, finally, tends to mainstream and normalize both radical right parties and their policies – although this does not have to be permanent (e.g. the Dutch PVV was excluded and marginalized again after withdrawing its support from the right-wing coalition government in 2012).

Exclusion by civil society organizations can limit the full mainstreaming of far-right organizations, at least temporarily, but, as many trade unions have found out, it does not prevent their members from supporting far-right ideas and parties. Moreover, while massive anti-racist demonstrations might have given solace and support to some of the targeted populations, who see that at least large parts of the population do not stand with the far right, they have not stopped the rise of populist radical right parties. And while anti-fascists can rightly claim some successes in the fight against the far right, not least owing to their (threats of) violence – for example, as noted in chapter 3, Richard Spencer abandoned his university speaking tour in the US in part because of anti-fascist violence – they also help to keep marginal far-right groups in the public eye, providing massive free media attention for their groups and ideas.

In the end, what works best depends on so many cultural and organizational factors that it makes little sense to look for a silver bullet. A political party like the Dutch PVV, with just one member, requires a different approach than not just a violent subculture like the US sovereign citizens, but also a political party like the Austrian FPÖ, which is deeply rooted in a centuries-old nationalist subculture. And a still relatively small opposition party in a consolidated liberal democracy, like the AfD in Germany, constitutes a fundamentally different challenge than a far-right president in a more fragile democracy, like Bolsonaro in Brazil. As such, if we are looking for a more effective response, the key probably lies in using different combinations of the existing approaches.

9

Gender

Like all political phenomena, the far right is deeply gendered. However, it is gendered in a much more complex manner than its often simplistic and stereotypical public image suggests. This should not be that surprising by now, given the heterogeneity of the far right that we have so far encountered. So, while it is true that men dominate the far right overall, there are more than enough exceptions, including female leaders like Marine Le Pen. And while traditional images of masculinity are central to many far-right groups and subcultures, think only of militias and skinheads, this is less the case in populist radical right parties in Northern Europe, for example.

This chapter looks at the importance of sex and gender in the various aspects that have been discussed in the previous chapters. Simply stated, sex is biologically determined, while gender is socially constructed. Sex is about men and women, gender about masculinity and femininity. Genders are socially constructed in a hierarchical and oppositional manner. Masculine traits are valued more than feminine traits and masculinity (strong) is defined in opposition to femininity (weak). As with all social constructions, gender is closely related to (sub)cultures, meaning that interpretations of femininity and masculinity will differ between and within countries. They are influenced by a host of different factors, including education, ideology, and religion.

The first section of this chapter looks at the different views of gender roles within the far right and discusses the importance of sexism. The second section looks at the representation of men and women according to the various *levels* (i.e. leaders, activists, and supporters) and their involvement in the different *types* of activities (i.e. elections, demonstrations, and violence) of far-right organizations. The last two sections look at the role of gender in the consequences as well as the causes of and responses to far-right success.

Ideology and Issues

The far right's views on gender (and sexuality) are, first and foremost, shaped by its nativism – be it ethnically or racially defined. Ideologically, the far right espouses a view that the German sociologist Andreas Kemper[1] has termed *familialism*: "a form of biopolitics which views the traditional family as a foundation of the nation, and subjugates individual reproductive and self-determination rights [of women in particular] to the normative demand of the reproduction of the nation."[2] Or, in the words of a leaflet of a local branch of the League in Italy, to celebrate International Women's Day no less, women have "a great social mission to fulfill in regard to the survival of our nation."

There are some important differences in the interpretation of familialism, however. Most far-right groups hold a traditional view on women, in which they are exclusively seen as mothers (or mothers-to-be). This means that women are discouraged from working, let alone from having a career. Instead, the state is to materially support non-working mothers and large families. Particularly in Western Europe, many far-right groups hold so-called "modern traditional" views on women, in which working women are tolerated, and even supported, but preferably after their child-rearing has ended. Many populist radical right parties in Northern Europe cannot even be described as modern traditional, given that they openly promote women's rights and don't prioritize motherhood. But their claim that gender equality has been achieved in their country betrays a relatively conservative outlook, at least within their national political context.

Traditionally, the far right mainly expressed so-called *benevolent sexism*, in which women are seen as morally pure and physically weak. This means that (good) women should be adored by men, as women are necessary to make men complete – through the heterosexual family, the heart of the nation or race. But it also means that women should be protected by (real) men, which is implicitly captured in the infamous "Fourteen Words" of one of the founding members of the neo-Nazi terrorist group The Order: "We must secure the existence of our people and a future for white children." He would later add fourteen more words: "Because the beauty of the White Aryan woman must not perish from the earth."

This means that views on both femininity *and* masculinity are very traditional. Real men work, preferably physical labor, and are aggressive and muscular, to protect "their" women. The family is heterosexual and male-dominated, in terms of authority and finances, although women are often ascribed a particular moral weight, which keeps the more aggressive, even animalistic, aspects of their men in check. First and foremost, however, the woman is the womb of the nation, the mother of children, responsible for morally and physically raising the next generation.

More recently, *hostile sexism* has become more overt within the far right, particularly online. Hostile sexism objectifies and degrades women, who are often viewed as trying to control men through feminist ideology or sexual seduction. Whereas benevolent sexism sees women as morally pure and physically weak, hostile sexism considers them morally corrupt and politically powerful. The growing prominence of hostile sexism within the far right is partly related to strong ties between the "manosphere" and the "alt-right." It is widespread within online subcommunities – from gamers (e.g. Gamergate) to "incels" (involuntary celibates) and "pickup artists" – where politicized rape fantasies are openly debated. But hostile sexism has also entered party politics, for example in the new Dutch party FvD, whose leader, Thierry Baudet, has supported "pickup artist" Julian Blanc's claim that women want to be "overwhelmed" and "dominated" by men.

Benevolent and hostile sexism have different views not just on femininity but also on masculinity. In benevolent sexism, the man is physically strong, muscular and powerful. He is not threatened by women. In contrast, in hostile sexism, men consider themselves to be threatened by women, even if mainly implicitly and politically, rather than explicitly and physically. But in certain online communities, men self-identify as "beta males," physically weak and unattractive to women, in contrast to the traditionally masculine "alpha male." These views are closely related to a combination of *toxic masculinity* – in which manhood is defined by violence, sex, status, and aggression – and *misogyny* – a hatred of women – which is omnipresent online but also offline.

Most far-right groups present some combination of elements of benevolent and hostile sexism, which is generally referred to as *ambivalent sexism*. While online "alt-right" groups primarily express hostile sexism, most populist radical right parties, particularly in Western Europe, mainly emphasize benevolent sexism in their official propaganda, even if leading members express hostile sexism towards women who do not live up to their sexist ideals – such as female advocates of (Muslim) immigrants, lesbians, and feminists.

Irrespective of their gender views, or form of sexism, virtually all far-right groups see contemporary feminism negatively. While many Northern European radical right parties speak positively of the original feminists, even they claim that feminism has gone "too far" or is no longer necessary, because gender equality has been achieved – although it is now said to be threatened by Muslim immigrants. Outside of Northern Europe, most far-right groups, but also many conservative groups, argue that feminists are an intolerant and oppressive group (so-called "femiNazis") that wants to control society by imposing "a new form of totalitarianism."

Feminism, like homosexuality, is portrayed as a (mortal) threat to the nation by many far-right groups. There are two, closely integrated, strands of this argument. First, feminism is claimed to undermine the traditional family and thereby the survival of "the nation" – a major concern of the far right in Eastern Europe, where countries are facing rapidly declining birth rates. Second, feminism is considered to be "alien" to the national culture, and often even portrayed as a "weapon" by which foreigners try to weaken the nation – quite often these foreigners are (mostly) Jews, like George Soros.

The other main threat to the nation, and especially its women, is seen as "alien" men. Far-right propaganda is filled with images and stories that play off the age-old western racist stereotypes of (Muslim and non-white) men as animalistic and hyper-sexual predators. Moreover, in line with so-called *femonationalism*, women and women's rights are claimed to be under threat of an "invasion" of Muslims and "Global Islam." As Marine Le Pen wrote in a January 2016 op-ed in the French daily *L'Opinion*, "I am scared that the migrant crisis signals the beginning of the end of women's rights." The far right increasingly targets "native" women in its propaganda, arguing that it is their only defense against "Islamization" and subsequent subjugation.

Similarly, many far-right groups are staunchly homophobic, opposing the "homosexual agenda" that is alleged to threaten the nucleus of the nation, the heterosexual family. When the Polish Supreme Court sided with an LGBTQ organization that was denied

Women of the Identitarian movement demonstrating against a planned refugee shelter in Graz, Austria. The banner reads "Protecting women means closing the borders." (Source: Johanna Poetsch/istock/2016.)

service by a print shop in 2018, the PiS minister of justice responded, "The Supreme Court in this case spoke against freedom and acted as a state oppressor by servicing the ideology of homosexual activists." Various far-right leaders have made homophobic remarks, including Brazilian president Bolsonaro, who said that he would be unable to love his son if he was gay and that he would "prefer that he would die in an accident," or Jean-Marie Le Pen, who said in a 2016 interview with *Le Figaro*, "Homosexuals are like salt in soup. If there isn't enough it's a bit bland; when there's too much, it's inedible."

But more and more West European radical right groups and parties accept homosexuality and homosexuals. Some organizations, such as the EDL in the UK and the AfD in Germany, have (un)official groups for their LGBTQ members, while a few even have openly homosexual leaders, like AfD co-leader Alice Weidel. These groups consider homosexuals a potential new electorate for their Islamophobic propaganda. Espousing so-called *homonationalism*, groups like the EDL or PVV argue that LGBTQ rights, which are defined as part of "national culture," are threatened by Muslim immigration and that the far right is the only one to defend them. As failed UKIP leader Anne Marie Waters tweeted: "I'm a gay woman who values my freedom, believe me, Islam is out to get me."

People and Actions

Although the typical far-right leader, if *he* even exists, is both male and hyper-masculine (see chapter 3), particularly within European populist radical right parties few still meet that stereotype in the twenty-first century. Leaders increasingly either are female or do not conform to traditional notions of masculinity.

Where older male leaders like Jean-Marie Le Pen or Jair Bolsonaro personified the stereotypical "political soldier," younger leaders like Gabor Vona (Jobbik) and Tom Van Grieken (VB) look more like eternal students or stereotypical ideal sons-in-law, often patient and smiling in interviews rather than angry and belligerent. Perhaps the most illustrative example of the new far-right man is Jimmie Åkesson, who stepped back as SD leader for several months in 2014 in order to battle burnout. Similarly, US "alt-right" leader Richard Spencer, whom mainstream media regularly praise for his fashion sense – the progressive US magazine *Mother Jones* described him as "an articulate and well-dressed former football player with prom-king good looks and a 'fashy' (as in fascism) haircut" – has openly expressed his disdain for physical confrontations.

In addition, there are more and more leading women within far-right groups and parties. Several populist radical right parties have (had) female leaders, including Alice Weidel (AfD), Giorgia Meloni (Brothers of Italy), Pauline Hanson (ONP), Pia Kjærsgaard (DF), Frauke Petry (AfD), and, of course, Marine Le Pen (RN). Other groups and parties have women within their leadership, like Barbara Pas (VB) and Magdalena Martullo-Blocher (SVP). While most parliamentary delegations of populist radical right parties have few women, although the percentage tends to go up when the total numbers of seats for the party increases, they are often fairly similar to other (smaller) right-wing parties.

As populist radical right parties largely reflect the sex bias and gender roles of conservative parties, many extreme right groups and subcultures are fairly similar to their non-far-right and non-political equivalents. For example, there are similarities in socio-demographics of "fascist" and "anti-fascist" groups as well as far-right and non-political skinheads – all predominantly younger and male. What is unique to the far right, however, is

Marine Le Pen speaks at a rally for the 2014 European elections under the slogan "Yes to France, No to Brussels." (Source: TV Patriotes/Flickr/2014.)

the gender gap in the membership and particularly the electorate, which is often roughly two to one or sixty–forty male-to-female. Populist radical right parties therefore have a much larger gender gap than all other parties, with the notable exception of Green parties (which are disproportionately supported by women). In contrast, Christian democratic and conservative organizations and parties tend to have slightly more female than male members and supporters – in part because women live longer and tend to be more religious.

Women are underrepresented on the far right not only in terms of voting, but also in terms of demonstrating and, particularly, using violence. While larger demonstrations, particularly of Islamophobic groups like the EDL and PEGIDA, can have a sizeable minority of female participants, most smaller demonstrations by extreme right groups are almost exclusively male. Women can be involved in far-right political violence, particularly in its usual, more spontaneous racist form, but very few are among the convicted perpetrators. Almost all premeditated far-right violence, including terrorist attacks, is committed by male lone wolves or small cells of men. A notable exception is Germany's National Socialist Underground, in which one of the three core members was a woman, although she was allegedly not personally involved in the murders.

Consequences

Until recently, we had little idea what the gendered effects of far-right rule would be, given that populist radical right parties were at best junior coalition parties in broader right-wing governments. They often shared their (modern) traditional gender views with their dominant, mainstream right coalition partners. Consequently, these governments did not stand out from other conservative ones. This is changing rapidly in the fourth wave, however, as more and more populist radical right parties come to power.

In Hungary, radical right prime minister Viktor Orbán has enshrined familialism in the new constitution, which asserts that Hungary "shall protect the institution of marriage as the union of a man and a woman" because the family is "the basis of the nation's survival." Similarly, the PiS government in Poland has adopted a policy of "family mainstreaming," which puts the heteronormative family at the core of "the political rules of the government."[3] In addition to the promotion of traditional gender roles, including by relatively generous state subsidies, staunch opposition to abortion is a key aspect of (far-right) familialism. So are attacks on groups and individuals promoting feminism (or homosexuality), who are depicted as "traitors" or "agents of a transnational lobby." Populist radical right governments in Hungary and Poland have actively targeted women's rights NGOs with new tax legislation as well as with raids of offices and arrests of activists. Unsurprisingly, many far-right groups, as well as many conservative groups, have targeted the academic discipline of Gender Studies, which they consider a "pseudoscience" that undermines the traditional family structure. Putting words into deeds, the Orbán government banned the two existing Gender Studies programs in Hungary in 2018, arguing that "people are born either male or female and we do not consider it acceptable for us to talk about socially constructed genders, rather than biological sexes." At the same time, the recently privatized Corvinus University has started an "Economics of Family Policy and Public Policies for Human Development" program, undoubtedly hoping to profit financially from the government's family mainstreaming agenda.

Similarly, far-right governments have undermined the position and rights of the LGBTQ community. Within hours of his inauguration, Brazilian president Bolsonaro, long known for his homophobic remarks, stripped LGBTQ concerns from the Human Rights Ministry and named Damares Alves, an ultraconservative pastor, as minister of women, family and human rights, and indigenous people. Alves argues that diversity policies have threatened the Brazilian family and that there will be "no more ideological indoctrination of children and teenagers in Brazil" under the new administration. "Girls will be princesses and boys will be princes." Many of these policies and views are also promoted by the Trump administration, although they are largely in line with existing Republican Party policies, and seen as more a priority of Vice-President Mike Pence than President Trump.

But the far right can also affect societal norms outside of parliament. Traditionally, far-right violence was strongly gendered. Consistent with benevolent sexism, and traditional views of masculinity, physical violence of the stronger male against the weaker female was frowned upon. Consequently, not only were perpetrators of far-right violence disproportionately male, so were their victims. To be clear, this applies exclusively to "political violence," given that "domestic violence" and sexual assault are serious problems within many far-right groups, including among leading members of populist radical right parties – one only has to think of Trump's infamous *Access Hollywood* tape, in which he brags about grabbing women by the pussy. Moreover, far-right men (and women) often and openly engage in verbal and even physical attacks on "native" women who associate with "alien" men – for many neo-Nazi and white nationalist groups, "race mixing" makes (mainly) women part of the "white genocide."

Given that hostile sexism considers women politically powerful, male violence against women has become more acceptable and frequent. This is particularly the case with verbal violence, but increasingly also with physical violence. For instance, in many "alt-right" online communities particular vitriol is reserved for women who do not live up to their misogynist standards. But more recently women have also become the prime target of physical violence by far-right incels. Most prominently, a twenty-two-year-old man killed six and seriously injured fourteen before committing suicide in Isla Vista, California, in 2014. The killer, who referred to himself as "The Supreme Gentleman," had distributed a 141-page document online hours before his attack, expressing his deep-rooted loathing of women and his intense frustration over his virginity. This not only made him into a hero within online far-right and incel communities, it also inspired several other deadly misogynist attacks, including the ones in Toronto, Canada, and Tallahassee, Florida, both in 2018.

Causes and Responses

Paradoxically, while men are overrepresented within the far right, almost all research on gender within the far right focuses on women. Similarly, while traditional gender roles and (benevolent or hostile) sexism are often mentioned as reasons for why women would feel less attracted to the far right, they are less often mentioned, and rarely elaborated upon, as reasons why men are more attracted. However, it makes sense that these gendered views play a bigger role in attracting men *to* the far right than in repelling women *from* it. After all, they blend in with other far-right ideological features, which believe in the superiority of the white (or major ethnicity) heterosexual male.

Similarly, the masculine image of the far right, portrayed by both its supporters and its opponents, will be disproportionately attractive to men – particularly less educated and older men. While many women, with similar characteristics, also hold traditional gender views, this masculine image will not necessarily entice them to become active within these groups. Moreover, the association of the far right with violence deters many women, but attracts certain men. Extreme right groups are often attractive to young men who desire a sense of martial camaraderie strengthened by (occasional) violent confrontations with anti-fascists.

Most far-right groups also mainly call upon men, rather than women, to become politically active. It is up to men to "secure the existence of our people and a future for white children." Extreme right groups portray *active* strong men as defenders of *passive* weak women. Some propaganda tries to mobilize men by attacking them for not protecting "their" women from murder and rape by "alien" men and even try to shame those not yet active by pointing out that, as a consequence of their (feminine) passivity, some women have to engage in (masculine) struggle. Populist radical right parties provide fairly similar messages in a more subtle and less violent manner.

In the far-right worldview, it is natural for men to be politically active. This is generally not the case for women. Consequently, far-right women often justify their political activism in terms of motherhood. They become members of far-right organizations because they are "afraid for the future of my children." Even several female far-right leaders use this traditional trope. Sarah Palin presented herself in the 2008 US presidential campaign as a "hockey mom," while Pauline Hanson saw herself as the mother of her nation, stating in 1998 that "Australia is my home and the Australian people are my children." But not only are far-right women more often reluctantly political, they also more often claim to be accidentally political. Interviews with activists of far-right groups and parties, in Europe and the US, find that almost all men claim to have made a conscious choice to become active, whereas a significant minority of women say it was because of a relative, or that they, more or less accidentally, ended up within the movement.

Just as benevolent sexism creates space for women as mothers, hostile sexism provides opportunities for women who meet its ideal of femininity. Female online "alt-right" stars like American Lana Lokteff (from website and TV station *Red Ice*) and Canadian Lauren Southern (formerly of *Rebel Media*) are young women who sell a far-right message through their image of a hyper-sexualized, Nordic beauty. Similarly, some of their male counterparts, like Lokteff's Swedish husband Henrik Palmgren and his countryman Marcus Folin (a.k.a. "The Golden One"), portray the traditional masculinity of the (mythical) Nordic Viking.

Unsurprisingly, given the large female support for mainstream right-wing groups and parties, sexism is not the main reason why women support the far right at (much) lower levels than men. Neither is the popular misperception that women are less nativist and authoritarian, or have a "natural" solidarity with other marginalized groups. Many surveys show that, in general, women hold largely similar views to men on crime, immigration, and terrorism, among many other issues. Consequently, when they support far-right parties, women do so for by and large the same reasons as men: opposition to immigration and concerns about crime and insecurity.

What sets female voters apart from male voters is their lower political self-confidence (efficacy) and their much lower tolerance for violence. In almost all national cultures, and subcultures, the far right is associated with violence – be it because of its actions, its self-presentation (clothes and symbols), or sensationalist media coverage. In much of the postwar era, even the non-violent populist radical right was considered outside of the political mainstream, ideologically and socially unacceptable. Consequently, even many women who hold authoritarian and nativist attitudes do not support far-right groups and parties either because of the (association with) violence or because they do not feel confident enough to support a socially unacceptable group.

This is changing, however. Women are increasingly becoming as politically self-confident as men. Moreover, during the fourth wave, the far right, and particularly the populist radical right, is increasingly mainstreamed and normalized. Many populist radical right groups and parties have "softened" their image, by using softer colors and symbols, more mainstream clothes and fashion, and more prominent women. The best example of this is the *dédiabolisation* (de-demonization) strategy of Marine Le Pen, who has barely moderated her party ideologically, but has provided it with a more "feminine" and therefore "softer" image. For instance, during her 2017 presidential campaign, she used only her first name Marine – trying to detach herself from the more extreme and violent reputation of her father – and used the symbol of a rose rather than the party's flame (which has strong fascist overtones).

There are, of course, risks to a more "feminine" image for far-right groups. While it might attract some, loosely committed, women, it could turn off more committed men, who are attracted to the far right exactly because of its "masculine" image. This is particularly the case for smaller extreme right organizations, like skinhead or neo-Nazi groups, which function more like a (criminal) gang than a (political) party for the mostly male members.

Given the partly different motivations for joining far-right groups, or (not) voting for populist radical right parties, of men and women, responses to the far right should include a gender perspective. For example, while highlighting the violent character of the far right could keep women from joining, it might make certain men keener to join. Similarly, some research shows that personalizing nativism and racism, by including detailed and personal experiences by the victims, is very effective with girls and women, but less so with boys and men. And exit programs for far-right activists have to think about alternative activities and groups that are attractive to boys and men who hold traditional interpretations of masculinity, but without strengthening them – let alone toxic masculinity. Finally, such programs need to address the sense of insecurity and nostalgia that underpins the male supremacy enshrined in, but largely obscured by, white supremacy.

10

Twelve Theses on the Fourth Wave

I want to finish this short book with twelve theses that illustrate and summarize the most important aspects and developments of the contemporary far right. Most of these are unique to the fourth wave of the postwar far right, which roughly started at the beginning of the new century, illustrating that we are dealing with a different political context than in the third wave of the late twentieth century. While the far-right phenomenon is roughly the same as in the third wave, at least in ideological terms, the political context in which it operates has changed dramatically – partly because of the actions of the far right, but mainly because of actions and developments outside of its direct impact.

1 The Far Right Is Extremely Heterogeneous

We often speak about *the* far right as if it is a homogeneous entity, identical within time and space. But the far right is plural rather than singular. It differs significantly on a broad range of factors, most notably ideology:

for example, the anti-democratic extreme right versus the anti-liberal democratic radical right. The far right mobilizes in different types of organizations (e.g. parties, social movement organizations, subcultures) and through various types of activities (e.g. elections, demonstrations, violence) – although several individual activists are involved in multiple types of organizations and activities. Some groups and subcultures are global, many are national, and most are only regional or even local. Moreover, there is no one-on-one relationship between type of ideology and type of organization: there are extreme right parties (e.g. XA) and radical right movements (e.g. PEGIDA).

But even within the most relevant subcategory of the far right, that is, populist radical right parties, differences are at least as pronounced as similarities. The parties differ in terms of age, electoral success, history and legacy, leadership, organization, and political relevance. There are poorly organized parties with an extreme right history and little electoral success, like the Portuguese National Renovator Party, but also well-organized, decades-old parties which are among the most successful parties in their country, like France's RN or India's BJP. They include parties that emerged on the extreme right, like Sweden's SD, as well as transformed conservative parties, like Fidesz and Switzerland's SVP.

2 The Populist Radical Right Is Mainstream(ed)

While the extreme right remains largely marginal and marginalized, the populist radical right has become mainstreamed in most western democracies. Mainstreaming takes places because populist radical right parties and mainstream parties address increasingly similar issues and because they offer increasingly similar issue positions. The change can come from movement by the populist radical right (moderation), by the mainstream (radicalization), or by both at the same time (convergence).

At the beginning of the third wave, populist radical right parties were seen as "niche parties" which mainly addressed socio-cultural issues like crime and immigration. In contrast, mainstream parties competed primarily on the basis of socio-economic issues like taxation and unemployment. But in the last two decades, socio-cultural issues have come to dominate the political agenda. In most European countries, as well as in Australia and the US, the political debate is dominated by socio-cultural issues and so-called "identity politics," including a more or less explicit defense of white supremacy in the face of the increasing politicization of ethnic and religious minorities. Consequently, socio-cultural issues are no longer niche as mainstream parties now also prioritize them over socio-economic issues, at least in their electoral campaigns. One could even argue that today socio-economic issues have become niche.

But mainstream and populist radical right parties not only address the same issues, they also increasingly offer similar issue positions. Research shows that this is the consequence more of the radicalization of mainstream parties than of the moderation of populist radical right parties. In fact, over recent decades, the populist radical right has barely moderated, not even when in government. Instead, mainstream parties have radicalized, moving further towards the (populist radical) right in terms of, first and foremost, immigration and integration, but also law and order, European integration (or international collaboration more generally), and populism.

The salience of socio-cultural issues like immigration and terrorism, as well as the radicalization of mainstream parties, is obviously related to specific political events, such as jihadist terrorist attacks and the so-called "refugee crisis," but it is important to remember that these events are politically framed: that is, the influx of more than a million asylum seekers to Europe in 2015 could have been debated as a humanitarian tragedy instead of a threat to national culture and sovereignty. Whereas many mainstream parties primarily adopted populist radical right discourse before, they are now increasingly adopting their frames and, therefore, policies too. This has significant broader consequences for contemporary politics.

As socio-cultural issues have come to dominate the political agenda, and mainstream parties have increasingly adopted the frames of the radical right, it comes as little surprise that populist radical right parties have increased not only their electoral support but also their political impact. In fact, in some countries they do not even have to be (officially) part of the government to dictate a significant part of its agenda, most notably immigration and integration policies, such as in the Czech Republic, France, or the UK. It is important to remember that this is taking place as populist radical right parties are still, in almost all countries, a political minority – on average the third biggest party in the country.

3 Populist Radical Right Politics Is No Longer Limited to Populist Radical Right Parties

As a consequence of mainstreaming, populist radical right politics is no longer (primarily) limited to populist radical right parties. Statements that used to be exclusive to populist radical right parties in the third wave have become "common sense" in the fourth wave. This started out relatively moderate. For instance, mainstream leaders from (then) French president Nicolas Sarkozy to German chancellor Angela

Merkel have stated that multiculturalism has failed, while (then) Czech president Václav Klaus and Dutch prime minister Mark Rutte have argued that European integration has gone too far and the EU has become a "bureaucratic moloch" that threatens democracy in the member states. In the US, (neo)conservatives in the Republican Party, including Texas senator Ted Cruz, were parroting far-right conspiracy theories about the UN (and the alleged "New World Order") well before President Trump brought them into the White House.

But decades of authoritarian and nativist responses to jihadist terrorist attacks, as well as the so-called "refugee crisis" of 2015, have led to a change not just in discourse, but also in policies. Many political leaders in Central and Eastern Europe have likened the "refugee crisis" to a Muslim invasion, some even calling for the monitoring of all Muslims in their country, while a majority of Republican governors in the US supported a "Muslim ban." Even countries that do not have a strong far-right opposition party, like Australia or Slovenia, have mainstream (right-wing) parties that advocate for strong nativist policies. In fact, Australia's brutal refugee policy has become an inspiration for populist radical right parties across Europe.

4 The Boundaries Have Become Blurred

One of the consequences of the mainstreaming of populist radical right parties, and the growing separation between policies and parties, is that the boundaries between mainstream (right-wing) and populist radical right parties have become increasingly porous. For instance, compared to their predecessors (the Union for a Popular Movement and the FN) in the third wave, the differences between France's Republicans and the RN in the fourth wave are marginal. Similarly, what makes parties like the Israeli Likud and US Republican Party mainstream right, but parties like the Danish DF or the Norwegian Progress Party populist radical right? These issues are even more pronounced in much of Eastern Europe, with parties like the Croatian Democratic Union, Latvia's National Alliance, or the Slovenian Democratic Party.

This is an important question, both morally and politically, and needs to be more openly and critically discussed in academic and public debates. For decades, the far right has been externalized, associated with amoral and marginalized groups. By definition, mainstream parties were not populist radical right and did not implement populist radical right policies. This meant that, mostly implicitly, it was assumed that the only challenge to liberal democracy came from outside, not inside, the political mainstream. It is clear that this can no longer be upheld. Many of the immigration policies that have been proposed, and even implemented, by mainstream parties, including of the left wing (e.g. the Hollande and Renzi governments in France and Italy, respectively), are virtually identical to those exclusively proposed by populist radical right parties in the third wave. They are steeped in an authoritarian, nativist, and/or populist worldview, irrespective of whether these mainstream parties have adopted them for opportunistic reasons or have truly transformed ideologically.

5 The Populist Radical Right Is Increasingly Normalized

It should come as little surprise that, as the boundary between mainstream and populist radical right politics becomes more and more blurred, the populist radical right is becoming increasingly normalized. To be clear, the extreme right is still mostly rejected, although even that is changing. For instance, Brazilian president Bolsonaro has openly flirted with military government, while US president Trump has defended "alt-right" protesters in Charlottesville. And the world's largest party, the Indian BJP, is part of a Hindutva subculture that includes openly extremist and violent groups. Nevertheless, in most cases, support for the extreme right within the political mainstream is either muted or, if voiced, still broadly opposed.

In sharp contrast, populist radical right parties, and particularly ideas, are increasingly tolerated, and even embraced, by business, civil society, economic, media, and political circles. This has reached new levels in the wake of Brexit and Trump in 2016, which saw an outpouring of understanding for "working-class voters" that was often framed within an outright populist narrative. The common people ("Somewheres") were the political victims of an out-of-touch elite ("Anywheres"). This frame is not just pushed in right-wing media, notably Murdoch-owned media in Anglo-Saxon countries, but also enthusiastically embraced by liberal media. Leaving aside that it reduces populist radical right support to the working class, which is empirically incorrect, it reduces the working class to just whites and nativists, another problematic simplification.

The argument that populist radical right voters are protest voters, rather than supporters of a radical right agenda, has been present since the beginning of the third wave in the early 1980s. What sets the fourth wave apart is that whereas they used to be portrayed as gullible and misguided, they are now increasingly portrayed as the voice of common sense. In populist terms, it is "the people" (reduced to radical right voters) who are "authentic" and "moral," and "the elite" (i.e. all mainstream parties) who are "cosmopolitan" and "corrupt." To be sure, this is not (yet) the dominant narrative, but it has made serious inroads in both conservative and liberal circles, including within academia.

6 The Extreme Right Are a Normal Pathology, the Populist Radical Right a Pathological Normalcy

During most of the postwar era, the far right was seen as a "normal pathology" of western democracy, that is, a premodern phenomenon, ideologically unconnected to modern democracy, and supported by just a small minority of the population. In reality, the so-called "normal pathology" thesis was always at best partly true. Overall, it did apply to the extreme right, as support for (open) racism and, particularly, non-democratic regimes was indeed limited to a small minority of the population in most countries.

The populist radical right, on the other hand, is much more a pathological normalcy, that is, a radicalization of mainstream values, supported by sizeable minorities, if not outright pluralities and majorities. Surveys from Austria to the US and Brazil to India show that large parts of the population hold authoritarian, nativist, and populist attitudes. Moreover, these attitudes are clearly related to mainstream ideologies and values, like anti-establishment sentiments as well as support for the nation-state and for law-and-order policies. This is not to say that the majority, or even plurality, of the populations in western democracies support a populist radical right ideology, or that there is no significant difference between the ideologies of mainstream and populist radical right parties. Rather, the difference is primarily a matter of *degree* rather than *kind*. The populist radical right does not stand for a fundamentally different world than the political mainstream;

rather it takes mainstream ideas and values to an illiberal extreme.

7 The Rise of the Populist Radical Right Is About Dealignment Rather Than Realignment (For Now)

When Green and New Left parties were making inroads into the political systems of Western Europe and North America, political scientists argued that we were experiencing a process of both dealignment and realignment. In other words, not only were people breaking their old ties to established parties (dealignment), they also were forcing new bonds with the Green and New Left parties (realignment). Similarly, many commentators have argued that the white working class has exchanged social democratic for populist radical right parties.

Despite remarkably high levels of loyalty among populist radical right voters in the 1990s, particularly for the FN and FPÖ, both parties suffered great losses in the early 2000s. And while they have bounced back since, it is clear that realignment is partial at best. More than half of the people who voted for Marine Le Pen in the first round of the 2017 presidential elections did not come out to vote for the FN in the legislative elections two months later. This is even clearer in the case of most other radical right parties, particularly in Central and Eastern Europe, whose support has been shown to be highly volatile – except for the conservative-turned-populist radical right parties in Hungary and Poland, which have been able to use state resources to keep their support base, at least for now. The consequence of this development is that, even if populist radical right parties return to electoral marginality in the near future (which is, however, unlikely), the party systems will not return to their stable origins.

8 The Far Right Is a Gendered Phenomenon

As with all political phenomena, the far right is gendered, but in a complex, multifaceted way. Most far-right groups are ambivalent sexist: that is, combining aspects of both benevolent sexism and hostile sexism. Even when they put "their" women on a pedestal, women who do not conform to benevolent sexist (in terms of reproduction or sexuality) or nativist/racist norms (by dating outside of their culture or "race") are met with virulent hostility. Similarly, while more traditional inter-pretations of masculinity predominate, in which men are expected to be strong protectors of weak women, toxic masculinity, in which mental and sexual frustration is taken out on independent and "opinionated" women, is increasingly prominent, particularly within far-right and related online communities (such as the "incels" and the "manosphere"). Toxic masculinity has also made women primary targets in some far-right political violence.

Almost all far-right groups subscribe to familialism, which sees women as mothers and, as such, as essential to the survival of the nation/race. Beyond that, far-right gender norms are mostly culturally determined. Almost all far-right groups hold more traditional gender norms within their own national cultural context. But the modern traditional views within the Northern European far-right groups, which support working women and often accept abortion and divorce, would be considered progressive in many Southern countries and are funda-mentally at odds with the traditional views of most far-right groups there, which see women exclusively as mothers.

Far-right propaganda is rife with femonationalism: that is, the use of women and feminist arguments (like gender equality) in support of nativism, in particular

Islamophobia. Women (and girls) are portrayed as vulnerable, threatened by "aliens" (domestic or foreign), and dependent upon the protection of "their" (masculine) men. It is only within the context of Islamophobia that far-right groups defend gender equality and women's rights, juxtaposing an egalitarian "West" against a misogynist "Islam." Given that they argue that gender equality has been achieved, even North European populist radical right parties tend to vote against gender equality policies, rejecting women's quotas as "tokenism," because "real women" don't need the state to protect their equality. In power, most far-right parties have tried to weaken feminist groups, and marginalize or oppose gender mainstreaming, instead creating and subsidizing a familialist, right-wing infrastructure.

The far right is still a predominantly male and masculine phenomenon in terms of leaders, members, and voters. This is particularly the case in smaller extreme right groups, in which a kind of martial camaraderie and an image and practice of violence attract a specific subset of men, while at the same time repelling most women. But things are changing. Female leaders are becoming more common and visible, don't always live up to the traditional image of femininity – this applies in particular to Marine Le Pen (RN) – while more and more male leaders are breaking with the traditional masculine image, like Jimmie Åkesson (SD) or Tom Van Grieken (VB). Given that the main reason for the underrepresentation of women within the far right is its association with violence, which is much more rejected by women than by men, this change in leadership, as well as the mainstreaming and "softening" of its propaganda, could make at least populist radical right parties more attractive to women – a still largely underutilized electorate.

9 No Country Is Immune to Far-Right Politics

For a long time, we have believed that certain countries or societies are immune to far-right politics. Americans and Brits claimed that their countries were exceptions, being inherently democratic, already having withstood fascist temptations in the early twentieth century. Dutch and Swedes believed their societies were so liberal that populist radical right parties could never take root there. And many believed that Germany had been so profoundly impacted by the Holocaust trauma and its impressive *Vergangenheitsbewältigung* (dealing with history) that far-right forces could never regain popular support within its repressive militant democracy. Similarly, commentators have long argued that the (fresh) memory of the right-wing authoritarian Franco regime explained the absence of a successful populist radical right party in Spain.

We now know that this was wrong. And even if there are still countries with unsuccessful far-right parties, like Canada or Portugal, this is more a supply than a demand issue. These countries have a fertile breeding ground for populist radical right politics too. They just have not yet been confronted with the right populist radical right party or political entrepreneur for their specific political context. How quickly this can change we are seeing in Spain, for example, where Vox has done what several other far-right parties before it failed to do. Admittedly helped by specific circumstances, including tensions around Catalonian independence and massive corruption scandals within the conservative Popular Party, Vox has rapidly achieved not just electoral success, but also political relevance.

10 The Far Right Is Here to Stay

The far right is here to stay. This even applies to the extreme right, which also survived the repressive aftermath of the 1945 defeat of the fascist movements and regimes that originally inspired it. To be clear, there are few indications that extreme right parties or politicians are returning to political power. Even in Greece, which probably resembles Weimar Germany more than any other democracy, the neo-Nazi XA is remarkably stable at roughly 5–7 percent of the vote. That said, extreme right actors and ideas have recently been praised by two of the most powerful men in the world, Brazilian president Bolsonaro (military dictatorship) and US president Trump ("alt-right" demonstrators in Charlottesville). Moreover, antisemitism and racism have returned to the center of the political debate, be it more implicitly in traditional media or more explicitly on social media.

In addition, there is a clear increase in both verbal and physical extreme right violence. Threats of violence by far-right activists and (anonymous) trolls remain commonplace on social media, although many platforms have recently become more repressive and vigilant, slowly but steadily tightening the virtual space within which the extreme right can operate. Both verbal and physical violence have exploded in the wake of the "refugee crisis," leading to insults and violence against both "aliens" and "natives" who are considered supportive of them. After decades of obsessing over jihadi terrorism, to the detriment of (other) domestic terrorist threats, many countries are increasingly warning against the growing threat of far-right terrorism. So far, most major attacks have been perpetrated by single attackers but even these individuals were tightly connected to the larger far-right virtual community.

Given that it is fundamentally related to mainstream values, albeit in a radicalized manner, and its more recent success is linked to structural changes and speaks to prominent issues, there is little reason to assume the populist radical right has reached its electoral or political peak. But while the support for populist radical right *ideas* within society is relatively stable, many populist radical right *parties* still have very volatile electorates. This is because the saliency of their *issues* is dependent upon the broader political context and varies in time and space. After all, politics is, first and foremost, local rather than global.

In the long term, however, the populist radical right is facing serious challenges. While its key issues – related to cultural, economic, and political integration – will remain relevant for some time to come, many societies are changing rapidly, becoming more diverse and more accepting of diversity. The US is expected to become a majority minority country within the coming decades, and while most European countries are nowhere near this, several of its major cities are. Moreover, while many populist radical right parties are profiting from resentment in the geographical periphery, as a new urban–rural divide has reasserted itself in many countries, most countries are still (sub) urbanizing, as the rural population is ageing and declining. Surveys show that younger generations and urban populations are much more accepting of the multicultural reality, which will make them less likely to support populist radical right ideas and parties. However, as long as younger people vote at much lower rates than older people, mainstream politicians will continue to cater more to the latter than the former.

11 There Is No Single Best Way to Deal with the Far Right

Given that the far right is highly diverse, there is no best way to deal with it. First of all, violent groups require a different strategy than non-violent groups. Dealing with the violent far right, which is predominantly extreme right, is primarily a law enforcement issue. Most countries already have the required laws on the books, and sufficient personnel in the state apparatus. What many lack is the willingness to acknowledge the threat of the far right and use their repressive resources to deal with it. Importantly, even violent far-right groups and individuals should be fought within the limits of liberal democracy, as excessive infringement of human rights and the use of force not only could create a violent backlash, but also would weaken liberal democracy as such, making the cure worse than the disease.

Non-violent far-right ideas and groups should be mainly addressed by educational and political initiatives. Given its limited support, the extreme right poses a much smaller challenge than the much more popular populist radical right. Neither pure exclusion, nor pure inclusion works. The former limits the liberal democratic space, while the latter weakens liberal democracy from within. Some argue that the best approach is to mix the two (cooptation), that is, exclude the groups but include the ideas, but developments in countries like Belgium and France show that this does little to stem the growth of populist radical right parties, while it makes their ideas and policies even more influential, given that they are now pushed by mainstream parties.

As the far right is always primarily a product of local and national conditions, the best way to deal with its challenge will always need to be developed in line with these conditions. For instance, whether you face a one-man party (PVV) or a mass party (BJP) has major consequences for how to construct a counter-response. Similarly, the far right poses a different type of threat in a parliamentary than a presidential system, or whether in opposition or in (coalition) government. This does not mean that each country, or locality, should reinvent the wheel. We can learn from each other, and across national and even continental boundaries. But, ultimately, the strategy should be local or national if it is to succeed.

12 The Emphasis Should Be on Strengthening Liberal Democracy

The ultimate goal of all responses to the far right should be the strengthening of liberal democracy. Put simply, only fighting the far right does not necessarily strengthen liberal democracy, but strengthening liberal democracy will, by definition, weaken the far right. That the two do not always go hand in hand is not always acknowledged. Limiting free speech or the right to demonstrate not only infringes on the democratic rights of far-right activists, it undermines these rights in general, and thereby the liberal democratic regime. This is not even to speak of the tendency for repressive measures aimed at one group to be later applied to other groups, including some that are neither radical nor right.

This is not the place to develop strategies in much detail. But let me suggest at least some guiding principles. First, we should be better at explaining why liberal democracy is the best political system we currently have, and how it protects *all* its discontents. To do this, we should be better informed, and more explicit, about the inherent tensions of the system, most notably between majority rule and minority rights. Second, we should develop and propagate positive political alternatives, based on a host of liberal democratic ideologies (i.e. Christian democrat, conservative, Green, liberal, and social democrat). Third, we should reclaim the political agenda on the basis of our own political programs. Rather than following the far right's issues, let alone their frames, we should address the issues that concern us, as well as the majority of the population, and posit our own, ideologically informed, positions. Obviously, this should not exclude any important issues, including those currently associated with the far right (like crime, corruption, and immigration). Fourth, we should set clear limits to what collaborations and positions are consistent with liberal democratic values – ideally *before* we are confronted with a significant far-right challenge. Only if we believe in liberal democracy can we defend it!

Notes

Introduction
1 The far-right parties in question are the Patriotic Front (Bulgaria), DF (Denmark), EKRE (Estonia), Fidesz (Hungary), the League (Italy), PiS (Poland), the SNS (Slovakia), and the Democratic Unionist Party (UK).
2 N. Bobbio, *Left and Right: The Significance of a Political Distinction*, University of Chicago Press, 1997.

Chapter 1 History
1 K. von Beyme, "Right-Wing Extremism in Western Europe," *West European Politics*, 11(2), 1988, pp. 1–18.
2 The Croatian Democratic Union transformed into a non-far-right party after the death of its powerful party leader, Croatian President Franjo Tudjman, in 1999. In more recent years, it has been one of several right-wing parties in the Western Balkans to be inspired by the illiberal turn of Viktor Orbán in Hungary.

Chapter 2 Ideology
1 For a more elaborate discussion of my terminology, see C. Mudde, *Populist Radical Right Parties in Europe*, Cambridge University Press, 2007.

Chapter 3 Organization
1 M. Minkenberg, *The Radical Right in Europe: An Overview*, Bertelsmann Stiftung, 2011.

2 See N. Higuchi, *Japan's Ultra-Right*, Trans Pacific Press, 2016.
3 From the SPLC website: *https://www.splcenter.org/ fighting-hate/extremist-files/ideology/alt-right.*

Chapter 4 People

1 M. Esser and J. van Holsteyn, "Kleur bekennen: over leden van de Centrumdemocraten," in J. van Holsteyn and C. Mudde (eds.), *Extreem-rechts in Nederland*. Sdu, 1998.
2 D. Albertazzi and D. McDonnell, *Populists in Power*, Routledge, 2015. I thank Duncan McDonnell for sharing some additional LN and SVP data with me.
3 See, respectively, Higuchi, *Japan's Ultra-Right*; and P.S. Forscher and N. Kteily, "A Psychological Profile of the Alt-Right," *PsyArXiv*, August 9, 2017.
4 See, for example, N. Mayer, *Ces Français qui votent Le Pen*, Flammarion, 2002.
5 E. Elkins, "The Five Types of Trump Voters: Who They Are and What They Believe," Democracy Fund, 2017, available at: *https://www.voterstudygroup.org/ publications/2016-elections/the-five-types-trump-voters.*

Chapter 5 Activities

1 F. Virchow, "Performance, Emotion, and Ideology: On the Creation of 'Collectives of Emotion' and Worldview in the Contemporary German Far Right," *Journal of Contemporary Ethnography*, 36(2), 2007, pp. 147–64 (p. 147).
2 J.A. Ravndal, "Right-Wing Terrorism and Violence in Western Europe: Introducing the RTV Dataset," *Perspectives on Terrorism*, 10(3), 2016, available at: *http://www.terrorismanalysts.com/pt/index.php/pot/ article/view/508/1008.*
3 See the paper by J.D. Freilich, S.M. Chermak, J. Gruenewald, and W.S. Parkin, "Far-Right Violence in the United States: 1990–2013," START, 2014, available at: *http://www.start.umd.edu/pubs/START_ECDB_FarRight Violence_FactSheet_June2014.pdf.*
4 I do not mention the names of far-right terrorists as

personal fame is one of the main motivations for their actions and creates a cult of personality that inspires potential other terrorists.

Chapter 6 Causes

1 See E.K. Scheuch and H.D. Klingemann, "Theorie des Rechtsradikalismus in westlichen Industriegesellschaften," *Hamburger Jahrbuch für Wirtschafts- und Gesellschaftspolitik*, 12 (1967), pp. 11–29.

2 I have developed the "pathological normalcy" thesis in more details in C. Mudde, "The Populist Radical Right: A Pathological Normalcy," *West European Politics*, 33(6), 2010, pp. 1167–87.

Chapter 7 Consequences

1 C. Mudde, "Three Decades of Populist Radical Right Parties in Western Europe: So What?," *European Journal of Political Research*, 52(1), 2013, pp. 1–19 (p. 1).

2 A.A. Ellinas, *The Media and the Far Right in Western Europe: Playing the Nationalist Card*, Cambridge University Press, 2010, p. 218.

3 R. Balfour et al., *Europe's Troublemakers: The Populist Challenge to Foreign Policy*, European Policy Center, 2016, available at: *http://www.epc.eu/documents/uploads/pub_6377_europe_s_troublemakers.pdf?doc_id=1714*.

Chapter 8 Responses

1 The categorization of party responses to the far right comes from M. Minkenberg, "The Radical Right in Public Office: Agenda-Setting and Policy Effects," *West European Politics*, 24(4), 2001, pp. 1–21.

2 On coalition formation with radical right parties, see S.L. de Lange, "New Alliances: Why Mainstream Parties Govern with Radical Right-Wing Populist Parties," *Political Studies*, 60(4), 2012, pp. 899–918.

Chapter 9 Gender

1 A. Kemper, *Foundation of the Nation: How Political Parties and Movements Are Radicalising Others in Favour of Conservative Family Values and Against Tolerance,*

Diversity, and Progressive Gender Politics in Europe, Friedrich Ebert Stiftung, 2016.

2 See W. Grzebalska and A. Pető, "The Gendered Modus Operandi of the *Illiberal* Transformation in Hungary and Poland," *Women Studies International Forum,* 68, 2019, pp. 164–72 (p. 167).

3 Ibid., p. 168.

Chronology

1948: MSI enters Italian parliament for the first time.

1951: ESM founded in Malmö, Sweden.

1952: SRP banned in Germany.

1956: National European Social Movement banned in the Netherlands.

Poujadists enter French parliament, including Jean-Marie Le Pen.

FPÖ founded in Austria.

1961: National Action for People and Nation founded in Switzerland.

1964: NPD founded in Germany.

1968: George Wallace wins five states in US presidential elections.

GRECE founded in France.

1972: FN founded in France.

1973: Progress Party enters Danish parliament for the first time.

Progress Party enters Norwegian parliament for the first time.

1977: Christoph Blocher becomes leader of Zurich branch of SVP.

US Supreme Court rules in the Skokie case.

1978: VB enters Belgian parliament as part of electoral list.

1979: VB officially founded as political party.

1980: BJP founded in India.

1982: Center Party enters Dutch parliament for the first time.

1984: Group of the European Right founded in European Parliament.

1985: XA founded in Greece.

1986: FN gains thirty-five seats in French parliament.

Jörg Haider becomes leader of FPÖ.

1987: B&H founded in the UK.

1988: SD founded in Sweden.

1989: Technical Group of the European Right founded in European Parliament.

SNS founded in Czechoslovakia.

1990: Franjo Tudjman elected president of Croatia.

SNS enters Czechoslovak parliament for the first time.

1991: LN founded as political party in Italy.

Greater Romania Party founded.

1992: RSS banned in India.

Liberal Democratic Party of Russia founded.

SNS enters coalition government under Vladimír Mečiar.

Greater Romania Party enters Romanian parliament for the first time.

Belgian parties introduce *cordon sanitaire* against VB.

1993: Ban against RSS in India lifted.

Liberal Democratic Party of Russia enters Russian parliament for the first time.

Greater Romania Party enters coalition government under Nicolae Văcăroiu.

B&H founder Ian Stuart Donaldson dies in car crash.

1994: LN enters coalition government under Silvio Berlusconi.

Kach party banned in Israel.

1995: MSI transforms into National Alliance.

DF founded as split from Progress Party in Denmark.

Far-right terrorist kills 168 people in bombing in Oklahoma City, US.

1996: BJP forms coalition government in India.

1997: ONP founded in Australia.

Japan Conference (Nippon Kaigi) founded.

1998: DF enters Danish parliament for the first time.

1999: National Union alliance enters Israeli parliament.

EDL founded in the UK.

2000: FPÖ enters coalition government under Wolfgang Schüssel.

Popular Orthodox Rally founded in Greece.

2001: LN returns to power in third Berlusconi government.

DF supports Danish right-wing minority government.

2002: Jean-Marie Le Pen qualifies for second round of presidential elections.

2003: CPI founded in Italy.

Identitarian Bloc founded in France.

Jobbik founded in Hungary.

2004: Flemish Bloc dissolved in Belgium, succeeded by Flemish Interest.

2005: Jörg Haider splits from FPÖ and founds Alliance for the Future of Austria.

2006: Geert Wilders founds PVV, enters Dutch parliament.

SNS enters coalition government under Robert Fico in Slovakia.

2007: Identity, Tradition, Sovereignty founded in European Parliament.

2008: Jörg Haider dies in car crash.

LN enters coalition in fourth Berlusconi government.

John McCain picks Sarah Palin as running mate in presidential elections.

2009: Tea Party launched in response to bailouts by US government.

2010: SD enters Swedish parliament for the first time.

Fidesz regains power in Hungary with constitutional majority.

Jobbik enters Hungarian parliament for the first time.

Far-right terrorist kills seventy-seven in Oslo bombing and Utøya shooting in Norway.

L'SNS founded in Slovakia.

EAF founded in European Parliament.

2011: Marine Le Pen becomes leader of FN.

Popular Orthodox Rally participates in government in Greece.

2012: Generation Identity founded in France.

XA enters Greek parliament for the first time.

EKRE founded in Estonia.

2013: Matteo Salvini becomes leader of the LN.

AfD founded in Germany.

Marian Kotleba elected governor of Banská Bystrica region in Slovakia.

Vox founded in Spain.

2014: PEGIDA founded in Germany.

BJP returns to power in India.

DF, FN, and UKIP become biggest national parties in European elections.

2015: Jean-Marie Le Pen expelled from FN.

EKRE enters Estonian parliament for the first time.

ENF founded; replaces EAF.

Frauke Petry becomes leader of AfD.

APF officially founded.

2016: Donald Trump wins presidential elections in the US.

Norbert Hofer (FPÖ) almost wins Austrian presidential elections.

UK votes to leave EU in referendum.

L'SNS enters Slovak parliament for the first time.

2017: "Unite the Right" rally in Charlottesville, Virginia.

Marine Le Pen qualifies for, and loses, the presidential run-off in France.

Alexander Gauland and Alice Weidel become co-leaders of AfD.

FPÖ enters coalition government under Sebastian Kurz.

2018: LN drops "Northern" and becomes League.

Jair Bolsonaro wins presidential elections in Brazil.

National Front (FN) is renamed National Rally (RN).

League enters populist government coalition under Giuseppe Conti.

Likud-dominated government passes Nation-State Law.

2019: Far-right terrorist kills fifty in attack at two mosques in Christchurch, New Zealand.

Vox enters Spanish parliament for the first time.

EKRE enters coalition government under Jüri Ratas.

Austrian government falls over FPÖ scandal.

Brexit Party, Fidesz, League, PiS, and RN become biggest parties in European elections.

Glossary

"Alt-right" "a set of far-right ideologies, groups, and individuals whose core belief is that 'white identity' is under attack by multicultural forces using 'political correctness' and 'social justice' to undermine white people and 'their' civilization" (Southern Poverty Law Center).

Ambivalent sexism a combination of benevolent sexism and hostile sexism.

Antisemitism hostility to or prejudice against Jews.

Authoritarianism the belief in a strictly ordered society, in which infringements on authority are to be punished severely.

Benevolent sexism the belief that women are morally pure and physically weak, deserving adoration and in need of protection by strong men.

Democracy a political system based on popular sovereignty and majority rule.

Ethnocracy a nominally democratic regime in which the dominance of one ethnic group is structurally determined.

Ethnopluralism the belief that people are divided into ethnic groups which are equal but should remain segregated.

Euroscepticism dissatisfaction about the process of European integration and the institution of the European Union.

Extreme right ideologies that believe that inequalities between people are natural and positive and that reject the essence of democracy.

Familialism the belief that the traditional family is the foundation of the nation and individual reproductive and self-determination rights are secondary to the reproduction of the nation.

Far right a combination of both the extreme right and the radical right.

Fascism a totalitarian ideology that offered a "Third Way" beyond liberalism and socialism based on economic corporatism, an ethical state, a national rebirth, an all-powerful leader, and the cleansing qualities and natural state of violence and war.

Femonationalism the use of women and women's rights in support of nativism, in particular Islamophobia.

Homonationalism the use of homosexuals and gay rights in support of nativism, in particular Islamophobia.

Hostile sexism considers women to be morally corrupt and politically powerful, trying to control men through feminist ideology or sexual seduction.

Islamophobia an irrational fear of Islam or Muslims.

Liberal democracy a political system that combines popular sovereignty and majority rule with minority rights, rule of law, and separation of powers.

Misogyny hatred of women.

Nativism an ideology that holds that states should be inhabited exclusively by members of the native group (the nation) and that non-native (or "alien") elements, whether persons or ideas, are fundamentally threatening to the homogeneous nation-state.

Populism a (thin) ideology that considers society to be ultimately separated into two homogeneous and antagonistic groups, the pure people and the corrupt elite, and which argues that politics should be an expression of the *volonté générale* (general will) of the people.

Racism the belief that people are divided into biological groups (races) which are hierarchically ordered.

Radical right ideologies that believe that inequalities between people are natural and positive and that accept the essence of democracy but oppose fundamental elements of *liberal* democracy.

Toxic masculinity defines manhood by violence, sex, status, and aggression.

Further Reading

The far right is among the most discussed political topics, and this is reflected in the wealth of available academic and non-academic literature. However, most focuses on radical right parties in Western Europe, while other groups and regions are much less covered. Very few, if any, books cover the full far right across the globe, as this book tries to do. What follows is a selection of some of the more accessible and useful (English language) literature on the topic.

Two excellent academic introductions to the topic are Jens Rydgren (ed.), *The Oxford Handbook of the Radical Right* (Oxford University Press, 2018), and Cas Mudde (ed.), *The Populist Radical Right: A Reader* (Routledge, 2017).

Jean-Yves Camus and Nicolas Lebourg, *Far-Right Politics in Europe* (Harvard University Press, 2017), provides a very broad overview of the **history** of the postwar European far right, while Andrea Mammone, Emmanuel Godin, and Brian Jenkins (eds.), *Varieties of Right-Wing Extremism in Europe* (Routledge, 2012), has a broad ideological and organizational scope too. Chip Berlet and Matthew N. Lyons, *Right-Wing Populism in America: Too Close for Comfort* (The Guilford Press, 2000), is the slightly dated, but still definitive, text on the history of the US far right. More encyclopedic overviews of the splintered US far-right scene are Betty A. Dobratz and Stephanie L. Shanks-Meile, *The White Separatist Movement in the United States* (Johns Hopkins University Press, 2000), and Stephen E. Atkins (ed.), *Encyclopedia of Right-Wing Extremism in Modern American History* (ABC-CLIO, 2011). For good introductions to the far right in Eastern Europe, see Michael Minkenberg (ed.), *The Radical Right in Eastern Europe: Democracy under Siege?* (Palgrave Macmillan, 2017), and Vera Stojarova, *The Far Right in the Balkans* (Manchester University Press, 2013).

An excellent introduction to the **ideology and issues** of the far right is Ruth Wodak, *The Politics of Fear: What Right-Wing Populist Discourses Mean* (Sage, 2015), which analyzes their discursive strategies. A broad-range analysis of far-right ideologies is provided by Gabriella Lazaridis, Giovanna Campani, and Annie Benveniste (eds.), *The Rise of the Far Right in Europe: Populist Shifts and "Othering"* (Palgrave Macmillan, 2016), while Sofia Vasilopoulou, *Far Right Parties and Euroskepticism: Patterns of Opposition* (Rowman & Littlefield, 2018), is the definitive study on far-right Euroscepticism. For the US, George Hawley, *Right-Wing Critics of American Conservatism* (Kansas University Press, 2016), is an encyclopedic intellectual history of the US radical right, while Mark Sedgwick (ed.), *Key Thinkers of the Radical Right: Behind the New Threat to Liberal Democracy* (Oxford University Press, 2019), highlights some of the key thinkers of the historical and contemporary far right.

The key texts on the **organization** of radical right parties are David Art, *Inside the Radical Right: The Development of Anti-Immigrant Parties in Western Europe* (Cambridge University Press, 2011), and Reinhard Heinisch and Oscar Mazzoleni (eds.),

Understanding Populist Party Organization: The Radical Right in Western Europe (Palgrave Macmillan, 2016). Duncan McDonnell and Annika Werner, *International Populism: The Radical Right in the European Parliament* (Hurst, 2019), analyzes the complex collaborations of far-right parties in the European Parliament, while Martin Durham and Margaret Power, *New Perspectives on the Transnational Right* (Palgrave, 2010), discusses a broad range of collaborations between European and North American far-right groups since the early twentieth century. The key book on CasaPound Italy is Caterina Froio, Pietro Castelli Gattinara, Giorgia Bulli, and Matteo Albanese, *The Hybrid Politics of CasaPound Italia* (Routledge, 2019).

Bert Klandersmans and Nonna Mayer (eds.), *Extreme Right Activists in Europe: Through the Magnifying Glass* (Routledge, 2009), provides great insights into the key **people** in West European far-right groups.

Most studies of far-right **mobilization** focus exclusively on (West) European *political parties*. The classic study is Hans-Georg Betz, *Radical Right-Wing Populism in Western Europe* (Macmillan, 2004). On far-right *movements*, see Donatella della Porta, Manuela Caiani, and Claudius Wagemann (eds.), *Mobilizing on the Extreme Right: Germany, Italy and the United States* (Oxford University Press, 2012), and Lawrence Rosenthal and Christine Trost (eds.), *Steep: The Precipitous Rise of the Tea Party* (University of California Press, 2012). Outside of Europe and the US, Naoto Higuchi, *Japan's Ultra-Right* (Trans Pacific Press, 2014), and Christophe Jalffrelot (ed.), *The Sangh Parivar: A Reader* (Oxford University Press, 2005), cover Japan and India, respectively. Max Taylor, P.M. Currie, and Donald Holbrook (eds.), *Extreme Right-Wing Political Violence and Terrorism* (Bloomsbury, 2013), provides a comprehensive overview of far-right *political violence and terrorism* in Europe and the US, while

José Pedro Zúquete, *The Identitarians: The Movement Against Globalism and Islam in Europe* (University of Notre Dame Press, 2018), is the definitive book on the Identitarian movement.

With regard to **subcultures**, George Hawley, *Making Sense of the Alt-Right* (Columbia University Press, 2017), Gary Armstrong, *Football Hooligans: Knowing the Score* (Berg, 2003), and Kevin Borgeson and Robin Valeri, *Skinhead History, Identity and Culture* (Routledge, 2017), are key texts on the "alt-right," hooligans, and skinheads, respectively. Cynthia Miller-Idriss, *The Extreme Gone Mainstream: Commercialization and Far Right Youth Culture in Germany* (Princeton University Press, 2017), is excellent on the importance of fashion in the mainstreaming of far-right culture, while Kirsten Dyck, *Reichsrock: The International Web of White-Power and Neo-Nazi Hate Music* (Rutgers University Press, 2017), covers the importance of white power music.

The key theories of the **causes** of the rise of radical right parties are concisely discussed and presented, within the British context, in Robert Ford and Matthew Goodwin, *Revolt on the Right: Explaining Support for the Radical Right in Britain* (Routledge, 2014). Other important theories are advanced in Mabel Berezin, *Illiberal Politics in Neoliberal Times: Culture, Security and Populism in the New Europe* (Cambridge University Press, 2009), and Jens Rydgren (ed.), *Class Politics and the Radical Right* (Routledge, 2013). For the US, the books by Kathleen Belew, *Bring the War Home: The White Power Movement and Paramilitary America* (Harvard University Press, 2018), and Christopher S. Parker and Matt A. Barreto, *Change They Can Believe In: The Tea Party and Reactionary Politics in America* (Princeton University Press, 2013), provide original explanations. On the role of the media, see Antonis A. Ellinas, *The Media and the Far Right in Western Europe:*

Playing the Nationalist Card (Cambridge University Press, 2010), and Nicole Hemmer, *Messengers of the Right: Conservative Media and the Transformation of American Politics* (University of Pennsylvania Press, 2016).

The study of the **consequences** of the far right is relatively recent. Some studies focus exclusively on specific policy effects of radical right parties, notably with regard to immigration, such as João Carvalho, *Impact of Extreme Right Parties on Immigration Policy: Comparing Britain, France and Italy* (Routledge, 2014). Other studies focus on the mainstreaming of European radical right parties, most notably Tjitske Akkerman, Sarah L. de Lange, and Matthijs Rooduijn (eds.), *Radical Right-Wing Populist Parties in Europe: Into the Mainstream?* (Routledge, 2015), as well as their impact on party systems, like Steven Wolinetz and Andrej Zaslove (eds.), *Absorbing the Blow: Populist Parties and Their Impact on Parties and Party Systems* (ECPR Press, 2018). Specifically on Eastern Europe, see Michael Minkenberg (ed.), *Transforming the Transformation? The East European Radical Right in the Political Process* (Routledge, 2015).

There are a growing number of studies of the **responses** to far-right politics, including William Downs, *Political Extremism in Democracies: Combating Intolerance* (Palgrave Macmillan, 2012), Erich Bleich, *The Freedom To Be Racist? How the United States and Europe Struggle to Preserve Freedom and Combat Racism* (Oxford University Press, 2011), and Bertelmans Stiftung (ed.), *Strategies for Combating Right-Wing Extremism in Europe* (Bertelmans Stiftung, 2010). An older text is Roger Eatwell and Cas Mudde (eds.), *Western Democracies and the New Extreme Right Challenge* (Routledge, 2003).

On the importance of **gender** within far-right groups, see the classic study by Kathleen Blee, *Inside Organized*

Racism: Women in the Hate Movement (University of California Press, 2002), and the more recent edited volume by Cynthia Miller-Idriss and Hillary Pilkington (eds.), *Gender and the Radical and Extreme Right: Mechanisms of Transmission and the Role of Educational Interventions* (Routledge, 2019), which also addresses the issue of sexuality. Finally, Michael Kimmel, *Healing from Hate: How Young Men Get Into – and Out of – Violent Extremism* (University of California Press, 2018), focuses specifically on masculinity.

For the best **journalistic accounts** of the far right, read Sasha Polakow-Suransky, *Go Back to Where You Came From: The Backlash Against Immigration and the Fate of Western Democracy* (Nation Books, 2017), and (the somewhat dated) Nick Ryan, *Homeland: Into a World of Hate* (Mainstream, 2003). Among the tsunami of new books on the US contemporary radical right, David Niewert, *Alt-America: The Rise of the Radical Right in the Age of Trump* (Verso, 2018), stands out for its depth and scope.

Some interesting **autobiographies** of former far-right activists include Christian Picciolini, *White American Youth: My Descent into America's Most Violent Hate Movement – and How I Got Out* (Hachette, 2017), Frank Meeink and Jody M. Roy, *Autobiography of a Recovering Skinhead* (Hawthorne, 2010), and Ingo Hasselbach, *Führer-Ex: Memoirs of a Former Neo-Nazi* (Random House, 1996).

Finally, there are several **academic and non-governmental organizations** that provide up-to-date information on far-right events, groups, and individuals, including:

Anti-Defamation League (ADL): *www.adl.org*
Center for Research on Extremism (C-REX): *www.sv.uio.no/c-rex/english*
Center for Right-Wing Studies (CRWS): *crws.berkeley.edu*

Hope not Hate (HnH): *www.hopenothate.org.uk*
Political Research Associates: *www.politicalresearch.*
   org
Southern Poverty Law Center (SPLC): *www.splcenter.*
   org

Index